What Indust

A practical and complete guide for those in the business of making exceptional memories. Connecting with nature is fundamental to our health and wellbeing and this Handbook helps to amplify the powerful benefits of nature by detailing how to create the ultimate visitor experience — words of wisdom for all nature experience providers!

Dawn Carr, M.A., M.P.A., Kinship Conservation Fellow
Executive Director
Canadian Parks Council
Ontario, Canada

++

A practical resource for operators tasked with leading organizations that not only fulfill their missions but also meet revenue goals. Consider using the strategies and techniques to audit your processes and management plan looking for ways you can enhance your team's efficiencies and effectiveness. You will not be disappointed.

Dr. John C. Crotts
Professor and Founding Chair
Hospitality and Tourism Management, College of Charleston
Charleston, South Carolina, USA

++

As someone who directed the tourism efforts of a well-known eco-sensitive destination situated on Lake Michigan for more than 30 years, I know that "setting the stage" is critical. This timely Handbook, authored by two top industry professionals, offers valuable insights to anyone who is charged with attracting visitors to natural, historical, or culturally-unique destinations.

Felicia Fairchild
Founding Executive Director
Saugatuck-Douglas Area Convention and Visitors Bureau
Saugatuck, Michigan, USA

The Ecotourism Provider's Handbook is filled with practical tips and steps to excellence. Donald and Vince have compiled 180 techniques and tips gathered from a career of service, research and observing visitors. From fundamental concepts to thought provoking ideas that will make a difference and have you excited about your organization's path forward. A must have Handbook and reference for Park and Recreation professionals everywhere.

Phil Gaines
South Carolina Director of State Parks, Retired
Professor of Practice, Parks Recreation and Tourism Management, Clemson University
Clemson, South Carolina, USA

++

Congratulations Donald and Vince on this well-crafted Handbook! The 180 techniques carefully elaborated in the Handbook should be found informative and useful by ecotourism experience providers as well as students and researchers in the tourism field. I highly recommend this practical and 'easy to read' Handbook!

Dr. Peter Kim
Associate Director of the New Zealand Tourism Research Institute
Auckland University of Technology
Auckland, New Zealand

++

The Ecotourism Provider's Handbook is a must-have for every new park ranger starting out at any ecotourism site. There is a myriad of helpful techniques, from training the 'again' effect to honoring the ten foot rule, that will undoubtedly assist new and existing staff foster top-notch visitor engagement. I only wish this Handbook were available to me years ago during my time as a park ranger with Florida State Parks—I would have referenced it on a daily basis!

Meghan Lauer
Workshop Coordinator, Natural Areas Training Academy
University of Florida
Gainesville, Florida, USA

The Ecotourism Provider's Handbook: 180 Techniques for an Exceptional Park, Preserve, or Nature-based Attraction is one of the most powerful tools that an outdoor recreational professional can have at their disposal. It provokes creative thinking, learning, and thinking outside of the box...

This book belongs at every staff meeting, it provides content for our conversations, it is a reminder of what to consider at the start of each project, it will be used as we refresh and improve old operations. It becomes a training manual for the newest employee and a refresher for all of us as we get caught up in the routine and forget how much fun and how easy it is to become outstanding.

Shawn Lindsey, MPA
Executive Director
Spearhead Trails
Southwest Virginia, USA

++

Donald Forgione and Vince Magnini have hit the mark with the Ecotourism Provider's Handbook. Whether you are a seasoned professional or just getting started, you will find the Handbook has exactly what you need to create an exceptional ecotourism experience. No stone is left unturned as Forgione and Magnini walk you through every detail of moving your park from good to great.

Jody Maberry
Former Park Ranger and Host of The Park Leaders Show
ParkLeaders.com
Port Townsend, Washington, USA

++

It's hard to imagine that anyone striving to enhance the quality of visitors' experiences in natural areas couldn't learn something enlightening from reading The Ecotourism Provider's Handbook. This authoritative yet easy to read reference manual contains a wealth of information and is an essential addition to the office of anyone involved in nature-based tourism.

Dr. Holly Ober
Associate Professor of Wildlife Ecology & Conservation
University of Florida
Gainesville, Florida, US

This is a must have Handbook for everyone working in the ecotourism industry. If you want to do things right, you go to the best and in the area of ecotourism, there are none better than Donald Forgione and Dr. Vincent Magnini. Dr. Magnini is a recognized world authority on maximizing the visitor experience and strategic planning while Donald Forgione has 40 years of proven hands-on experience and innovation, including running the award-winning Florida Park Service, acknowledged as the best in the nation. This Handbook is packed with little-known but invaluable techniques that will elevate your business to the next level and beyond.

Don Philpott
President
Florida State Parks Foundation
Tallahassee, Florida, USA

++

Who would have thought a Handbook would be a "page turner"? The Ecotourism Provider's Handbook provides page after page of creative ideas that result in delivering high quality tourism opportunities in a fun and easy to read format. It's essential for existing providers, and I look forward to using it in my university courses to train future providers.

Dr. Taylor V. Stein
Professor of Ecotourism and Natural Resources Management
School of Forest Resources and Conservation, University of Florida
Gainesville, Florida, USA

++

"Knowing is not enough; we must apply. Willing is not enough; we must do" (Johann Wolfgang von Goethe). The 180 techniques with assignments are a great way to prepare for a career in ecotourism. Well done! I am looking forward to applying the knowledge in my own professional field. Thank you very much.

Dr. Erika Quendler
Federal Institute of Agricultural Economics
Rural and Mountain Research
Vienna, Austria

There has been a rich stream of articles, books, cyclopedias, and reports on ecotourism in different settings over the past three decades or so. However, there is a gap in the literature for a book that solely focuses on the needs of ecotourism providers. Finally, we have a timely book 'The Ecotourism Provider's Handbook: 180 Techniques for an Exceptional Park, Preserve, or Nature-Based Attraction" that brings together 180 techniques, which are not known widely in nature-based attraction settings. if practiced, these techniques can not only differentiate you and your portfolio of product offerings but also enable you to sustain your competitive edge in the marketplace. It is a must have book for anyone who is managing and providing nature-based products and services.

Dr. Muzaffer Uysal
Professor and Chair
Hospitality and Tourism Management, University of Massachusetts
Amherst, Massachusetts, USA

++

This easy-to-read, comprehensive guide for the ecotourism provider includes a wide range of techniques for engaging the people who visit your site--as well as the larger community, whose welcome matters. Team managers will appreciate the practical approach and "assignments" for each technique to help move in the right direction.

Jennifer Wampler
Trails Coordinator
Virginia Department of Conservation and Recreation, USA
Richmond, Virginia, USA

++

Forgione's and Magnini's Handbook provides a rich, comprehensive and 'must have' set of readings for operators in nature-based settings. The authors have assembled a fine collection of contributions that help ecotourism providers frame, understand, and respond to key issues about how to operate an ecotourism site. This book sets a benchmark in the field and the authors are to be congratulated for their vision in creating this Handbook.

Dr. Anita Zehrer
Head Family Business Center
Head of Research Management & Society, MCI Management Center Innsbruck
Innsbruck, Austria

The Ecotourism Provider's Handbook

The Ecotourism Provider's HANDBOOK:

180 Techniques for an Exceptional Park, Preserve, or Nature-based Attraction

Donald V. Forgione

and

Vincent P. Magnini, Ph.D.

ISR | Publishing Division

Copyright © 2020 ISR Publishing. All rights reserved.
ISR Publishing Division
5780 SE 12th Lane
Gainesville, FL 32641
USA

All rights reserved. With the exception of brief quotations of 400 words or less, no part of this publication may be reproduced, stored in a retrieval system, or transmitted in any way by any means, electronic, mechanical, photocopy, recording or otherwise without the prior permission of the authors except as provided by USA copyright law. Enquiries concerning reproduction outside these terms should be sent to the publisher.

Efforts have been made to publish reliable information in this book. Nevertheless, neither the authors or publisher can assume responsibility for the validity of all materials or for the outcome(s) of their application(s).

Some of the statements in this book that are not historical facts are "forward-looking statements." Such forward-looking statements are associated with certain risks and uncertainties which could cause actual outcomes to differ from those predicted (explicitly or implicitly) in this book.

Registered trademarks of products, entities, or corporate names are used in this book only for explanation and identification without intent to infringe.

Published in the United States of America
ISBN: 978-1-7350350-0-0

TO INQUIRE ABOUT BULK ORDER DISCOUNTS: Call ISR Publishing at (352) 214-3277

Thank you for your love and support.

Rosie, Joey, Sage, Venus-Blue, and Vernon

Michelle, Demi, and Olivia

Dedicated

to the women and men worldwide who are protecting the natural resources, preserving historic sites, celebrating cultural heritage, and enriching the lives of visitors to these sites.

Contents

Purpose of this Book	13
Section I: Setting the Stage for the Visitor Experience	15
Section II: Fostering Top-Rate Visitor Engagement	39
Section III: Recruiting, Selecting, and Motivating Your Team	65
Section IV: Attracting Visitors to Your Site	91
Section V: Caring for Your Site's Ecosystem	115
Section VI: Keeping Visitors Safe	139
Section VII: Maximizing the Operational Efficiencies of Your Site	165
Section VIII: Engaging with External Audiences	191
Concluding Remarks	215
References and Notes	217
Index	228

The Purpose of this Book

This Handbook is intended for operators in nature-based settings who want to go from good to great. This Handbook is not an A-to-Z manual about how to operate an ecotourism site. Instead, it contains 180 techniques that are not widely known in parks, preserves, and nature-based settings, but if practiced can differentiate you and your offerings.

Why 180?

It takes 180 degrees to redirect a course of direction; hence, 180 techniques. Think of each technique as a degree on a compass and using just a few can alter your course for the better. Each page of this Handbook that offers a technique also recommends a particular assignment that will aid you and your team in implementing the given technique. For best results, the techniques should be read and evaluated by the group of individuals that comprise your operational team.

It is important to note in this introductory section that this Handbook is designed for use by all types of ecotourism experience providers – including, for example, government conservation land managers, contractors, and vendors. Whether you are a helicopter, kayak, canoe, rock climbing, hot air balloon, fishing, hunting, bus, or sightseeing operator, there are tips in this book that can likely help you improve your operation.

Students and researchers aspiring for careers in ecotourism will also benefit from this Handbook. Learning the techniques before entering the field will aid in jumpstarting your career progression. Moreover, the latest research surrounding these techniques is synthesized in the reference section of this Handbook which facilitates additional research that readers may wish to conduct on a given topic(s).

In summary, there are multiple channels through which readers can extract value from this Handbook. Enjoy!

Section I

Setting the Stage for the Visitor Experience

Many of us are drawn to this line of work because of our love of nature. We often find ourselves asking questions about nature, and the more we learn, the more we want to know. When entrusted with natural resources, we feel both the honor and gravity of the responsibility of doing all that we can do to protect them. We often witness that people protect what they know and, therefore, we want to introduce as many people as we can with the land that we love. The art of arranging and managing a site's tangible assets is an important aspect of land management strategy. Knowledge shared with passion is felt not just seen or heard. We realize how important the visitors to the sites are, and we want to encourage even more to visit.

Some theater productions have many acts, and all of them play a role in the overall story. The stage production elements help create the mood and set the scene. This section presents techniques that are subtle to most visitors and may not even be consciously recognized by them. However, without strategically setting the stage and thoughtfully providing amenities visitors want, the story may be harder to tell, and an opportunity to spread passion and love of the land may be lost.

It is recommended that, as you read this section, you think of other ways you and your team can engage visitors, so they are relaxed and comfortable within your operation. Discuss with your team how you can further immerse visitors in the resources you are providing.

1	2	3	4	5	6	7	8	9	10
11	12	13	14	15	16	17	18	19	20
21	22	23	24	25	26	27	28	29	30
31	32	33	34	35	36	37	38	39	40
41	42	43	44	45	46	47	48	49	50
51	52	53	54	55	56	57	58	59	60
61	62	63	64	65	66	67	68	69	70
71	72	73	74	75	76	77	78	79	80
81	82	83	84	85	86	87	88	89	90
91	92	93	94	95	96	97	98	99	100
101	102	103	104	105	106	107	108	109	110
111	112	113	114	115	116	117	118	119	120
121	122	123	124	125	126	127	128	129	130
131	132	133	134	135	136	137	138	139	140
141	142	143	144	145	146	147	148	149	150
151	152	153	154	155	156	157	158	159	160
161	162	163	164	165	166	167	168	169	170
171	172	173	174	175	176	177	178	179	180

Technique #1

Provide a Welcoming Entrance

In many operations, there is often a short stretch of road between the highway or other government-maintained roads and the first contact facility within your operation. This should be the "Welcoming Section" of the entrance road as the visitor enters your operation and the "Thank You Section" as the visitor subsequently departs. Signage in these areas should be limited and have only the necessary messaging to welcome and thank the visitor and convey only information that is necessary before they arrive at the contact facility.

SETTING THE STAGE

Assignment

Review these sections of roadway and consider eliminating, reducing, or moving all signs that are not welcoming or do not communicate gratitude for visitors to your operation. If there are not any signs conveying these concepts, consider adding them to this section of the roadway.[1]

Technique #2

Know What People and Pets Often Need to Do Upon Arrival

Some operations are located far from the nearest town. The drive could be quite long for guests. Once the visitors arrive, they may have to park their vehicles and register or continue further into your operation until they finally can relax. In practicality, however, often the first thing that many guests need to do upon arrival is use the restroom facilities.

SETTING THE STAGE

Assignment

Make available as soon as feasible an area to relax including a restroom. When expanding or remodeling your operation, insist on adding a public restroom to the first building the visitors reach in your operation. If pets are allowed, consider a pet walking area as well with ample pet sanitation stations.

Technique #3

Use Consistent Materials and Branding on Signage

Signs are a component of your attraction's brand-related trade dress.[1] Consult with your staff and your sign provider and create a sign theme template that will thread throughout your operation. Select wood, aluminum, plastic, or other sign material that will be easily maintained in your environmental conditions. Choose colors, letter font, size, and sign shape for both interior and exterior applications.

SETTING THE STAGE

Assignment

Take photos of three interior and exterior signs and compare them for consistency to the desired theme. Adhere to a sign theme that is visually consistent with your brand and marketing efforts. Critically study the materials your signs are currently made of and every color that makes up each sign to determine if they are the best choice when considering maintenance and color fading.

Technique #4

Create Well-Written Signs

When visitors come into your operation, they often are looking for an escape from their everyday regulatory lifestyle. No alarm clocks, no schedule, and no sign telling them how to behave. Some signs need to be made in a regulatory style like a speed limit sign or a caution sign. But some signs can be changed to soften the tone and still get the point across. For example, "No Parking on Road Shoulder" could be changed to "Road Shoulder Will Not Support Weight of Vehicle", if this is indeed true.

SETTING THE STAGE

Assignment

Select 3 regulatory styled signs within your operation and rewrite them to an informative Style. Consider informing the visitor of the "condition" and not how to "behave" to the condition. Share with your staff for input. If signs are changed, monitor for visitor compliance.

Technique #5

Manage Sign Mounting Height

Non-regulatory signs should be mounted at a minimum distance from the ground, so the sign does not distract from the visitor's experience but remains effective. An idea is to install signs, not regulated by law, so the bottom of the sign is no more than two feet from the ground. This low-profile concept will provide better opportunities for your visitors with regard to the vistas they are desiring to view.

> SETTING THE STAGE

Assignment

Measure the distance from the bottom of the sign to the ground for three of your signs. Compare your measurement to the recommendation. If two feet will not work in your operation, choose a distance to be consistent and share this information with your staff.

Technique #6

> **Maintain Well-Marked Trails**

In many outdoor recreation venues, the most common visitor activity is hiking. The most frequent hiking-related complaint is poorly marked trails and/or maps that do not match the trails. These wayfinding issues are at the forefront because visitors often have an inherent fear of getting lost in the wilderness. Consequently, any providers with trails should invest considerable attention in updating / maintaining trail signage and refreshing trail markers. Similarly, trail maps should be reviewed to verify that the maps are in concert with the signage (and vice versa).

It is important to note that trail signs and markers can sometimes be damaged or missing for an unreasonable amount of time because a staff member does not regularly hike the trails. Moreover, a trail can be amended through the years, for any number of reasons, but the map may not depict the new route.

> SETTING THE STAGE

Assignment

Have your staff hike the trails and ask them to take a photo of each sign and every location where they believe there should be one. They should note the photo locations on a trail map, preferably using a GPS waypoint. In doing so, they can also refresh any painted trail markers. Maps should also be reviewed to the GPS waypoints for accuracy.

Technique #7

Understand the Critical Role of Restroom Cleanliness

One of your most important facilities in your operation is your restrooms.[2] This is not only a hygiene issue but also a dignity issue and is often the topic of compliments or complaints by visitors. The day-to-day cleaning needs to be a high priority for staff. Any out of order fixture should be repaired immediately.

SETTING THE STAGE

Assignment

Create a culture that embraces restrooms as a dignity issue. Train staff that the goal is to provide clean and functional restrooms 100% of the time. To enhance restroom experience, choose light colored walls, stall partitions, as well as ceilings and floors that will present a clean bright appearance.

Also regarding restroom cleanliness, in camping areas (although it is not a sanitation / hygiene issue), if a spider web, mud dauber, or other insect residue is permitted to remain on the ceiling or upper-wall, visitors will perceive that the restroom has not been cleaned since their previous visit.

Technique #8

Maximize Natural Screening

Visitors to ecotourism sites do not want to view aesthetically displeasing storage, maintenance, or staff break areas at the attraction. Often, such areas can be effectively screened from visitor view by growing, installing, or transplanting native vegetation or other natural materials to visually block these areas. The word "maximize" is used in the title of this technique because most ecotourism sites already do this to a certain extent, but such efforts can be improved at many sites.

SETTING THE STAGE

Assignment

Members of the team should move through the attraction using the same flows as potential visitors and ask: Are there any storage, maintenance, or staff break areas visible? If so, what can be done to increase the natural screening of these areas?

Technique #9

| **Install Useful and Visually-Consistent Fencing** |

Fencing can be an important tool to delineate the boundary of your operation and for managing your visitors' movements within your operation. There are many styles and materials to choose from. Select a style consistent with your site's theme and material that will be easily maintained given your environmental conditions. Fences can also be as attractive as they are useful if carefully considered.

SETTING THE STAGE

Assignment

Take photos of all the fence sections within your operation that visitors can see. If your operation is like most, you will find more than one style and material for no explainable reason. Make a written plan of your decision so when the time and materials are available, you can make your plan a reality.

Technique #10

Manage Buffer Zones

All sizes of operations need to realize the benefits of sight and sound buffer zones. These are designated areas that buffer the sight and noise of one use from another. The size of each zone is related to the activities on either side. A buffer may be large surrounding your operation from neighboring properties and perhaps smaller between internal uses.

SETTING THE STAGE

Assignment

Map out usage areas within your operation and determine if one activity is affecting another. For instance, are the headlights from vehicles affecting the stargazing potential in an adjacent area? Establish a plan to maintain or create buffer zones.

Technique #11

Create a Telephone Charging Station

Recharging electronic mobile devices can be a challenge while traveling and even more so in a remote ecotourism destination. Recharging cords are an easy item to accidentally leave at home, in a vehicle, or in a cabin. This is becoming more of an issue as we become more dependent on these devices.

> SETTING THE STAGE

Assignment

Buy a wireless charging pad or at least one of every type of recharging cord and create a "charging station" in the visitor center, check-in, or other convenient location within the operation. Inside a building and near a staff member's work area is preferable.

Technique #12

Understand the Prominent Role of Accessibility

There are obvious challenges for both the visitor to, and the provider of, nature-based attractions providing universal access to all areas of an operation. When it comes to providing accessibility, it is the attitude of the provider and not the disability of the visitor that sometimes defines the limits of accessibility. Consequently, it should be understood by providers that universal access should be offered whenever possible because it is a leading determinant of visitor satisfaction to many sites.[3] Even some visitors that appear able-bodied have various heart, lung, orthopedic, or other impediments that deem negotiating stairs, steep hills, etc. very challenging.

SETTING THE STAGE

Assignment

Discuss with the team what measures can be taken to make the attraction more accessible to those with health or mobility impediments. Can some of the site's physical features be amended? Can better systems be in place for communicating or offering assistance to visitors? Can live stream video feeds be used to help deliver places to those who cannot access them? For instance, it may not be possible to install an elevator in a historic lighthouse.

If a site is already highly accessible, is this feature adequately communicated on the website? Websites such as ADA.com may be of assistance to your team.

Technique #13

Have a Long-Run Parkitecture Plan

Parkitecture can be described as the art of designing a facility that is architecturally functional for both visitors and staff but as park-like as possible. A notable example of this concept are the facilities built in the United States by the men of the U.S. Civilian Conservation Corps (CCC) between 1923-1942.[4] Parkitecture within an operation is usually designed using an established theme that runs through many aspects of the operation. For example, after a floor plan is created, the façade can use the local building vernacular and local materials. The test should be that a visitor looking at one of your facilities should know that s/he is in your operation.

SETTING THE STAGE

Assignment

Photograph each building within your operation and compare each photo with the other. Look for roof type, color discrepancies, and architectural style variations. Develop a plan to have all buildings in your operation architecturally consistent with each other. Keep the plan in a safe location as this is a long-term project.

Technique #14

Have Easily Accessible Temporary RV Parking Available

RV camping continues to increase in popularity, while simultaneously the camping rigs also increase in size.[5] During check-in times, older facilities simply cannot accommodate the temporary parking required for checking-in. Blocking vehicular traffic because easily accessible temporary parking is not available is not only frustrating and embarrassing for RV guests but can also be frustrating for guests in other vehicles.

SETTING THE STAGE

Assignment

To reduce the potential bottle neck of camping rigs and improve the first impression by your visitors and your operation, create additional temporary parking. The design needs to be carefully thought out so the drivers of these RV camping rigs can easily park, check-in, and readily ease back on the road to your campground.

Technique #15

Install RV Pull-Through Sites or Remove Obstacles

RV camping rigs are large vehicles that require considerable driving skill to effectively operate. "Backing up" is one of the most common challenges drivers face. Therefore, when new sites are developed, whenever possible, design pull-through sites which can be entered and exited without ever needing to place the RV in reverse.

Where pull-through sites are not feasible, as many obstacles as possible should be eliminated. That is, there are situations where the campsite is large enough to accommodate the camping rig but because of a tree, boulder, or other obstacle on the opposite side of the campground road, a driver may not be able to navigate around the obstacle to successfully back into the site.

SETTING THE STAGE

Assignment

During the off-season when most of the campsites are available, ask a camper with a large RV rig to attempt to back into each site. Have staff watch on all sides for potential obstacles. Flag each identified obstacle and consider removing the obstacle to increase the success rate of large RV rigs backing into your campsites.

Technique #16

Have Loaner Wagons Available

Wagons and small push carts are handy for mostly overnight visitors to transport their belongings around specific designated areas of your operation. The distance from a facility or a parking area to the boat docks, campgrounds, and lodges could be a logistical challenge. These carts can transport groceries, firewood, laundry, and more.

SETTING THE STAGE

Assignment

Look for ways to incorporate the use of wagons and small push carts into your operation. Seek-out commercial or industrial grade items for function, maintenance, and overall investment. This will add one more amenity to your operation and a great personal touch for visitors.

Technique #17

Have Loaner Binoculars Available

When facilities are designed well, they often offer visitors spectacular views; whether they are from your visitor center, observation tower, or a roadside pull off. If such views are available at your attraction, encourage your visitors to enjoy loaner binoculars. This will especially be important to those that might not be able to go further into your operation.

SETTING THE STAGE

Assignment

Offer "loaner" binoculars to visitors. Take care to have child-friendly binoculars as well. Choose quality items that truly work well and are durable. If binocular "loss" is of concern, ask the visitors to temporarily hold their driver's license in exchange for the binoculars.

Technique #18

Create a Branded Photo Frame

Create a large lightweight photo frame branded with the name of your attraction that visitors can choose to hold-up and "frame themselves" when taking pictures. If the portable frame might be an issue, anchor the frame with a post to the ground. Visitors can then be encouraged to share the photos on social media.

SETTING THE STAGE

Assignment

Discuss with the team how the logistics of implementing this tactic would work at your attraction. Making it fun and aesthetically appealing will draw your visitors to it. If a permanent frame is chosen, select the placement with a great background without distracting the view for others.

Technique #19

Consider Maximizing Current Viewsheds

Trail signs leading to "one of a kind views" is smart management. Once there, signs should be limited to interpreting the view and any safety concerns. Signs or interpretive panels should be as low to the ground as possible while still being effective. Other park amenities should be strategically placed not to interfere with the visitors' view.

> **SETTING THE STAGE**

Assignment

Take a photo of your scenic views from as far back as possible. Count the number of signs in the photo and determine effectiveness. Consider eliminating, reducing, or moving the signs for an optimum view. If other manmade items are in the photo such as benches and trash receptacles, try to move them to other locations.

Technique #20

Plan for Future Viewsheds

If you are building a one-story structure with a view, consider planning the engineering of the structure to support an eventual second level. Too often, when ecotourism enterprises expand, they must construct a second one-story building because the original building cannot support a second level. The result is two buildings with mediocre views rather than one building with exceptional views.

SETTING THE STAGE

Assignment

When designing a building within your operation, consider more than your current needs and budget. Funds available often limit our imaginations. Ask yourself, "If I had no financial limitations, what would be the greatest design of this facility." Then design your dream for tomorrow and build what is feasible today.

Technique #21

Offer Activities with a Broad Spectrum of Difficulty Levels

Many of your visitors are likely physically fit and ready for the eco-adventures you are providing. However, some travelers are visiting with limited mobility or physical limitations. Moreover, in some cases, visitors will want to participate in the activities with their small children. Therefore, a balance of activities and degrees of difficulty should be considered so no one is left behind.

> SETTING THE STAGE

Assignment

Describe in writing the degree of difficulty or the skill set recommended for each activity you offer. For instance, a trail could be described as arduous while another trail could have elevations that may cause breathing issues. An alternate trail may be recommended for beginners. Review all the degrees of difficulty and try to have at least one activity per level. If a level is not currently offered, consider adapting a current activity or adding a new activity.

If it is a hiking or biking trail that you are recommending, you can refer to the crowd-sourced difficulty ratings on various websites such as www.AllTrails.com.

Technique #22

Bring In Fresh Eyes

Even a staff member with years of experience can overlook some issues or can learn a new technique to better the operation. Staff can walk by the damaged sign or paint peeling from a fence for years. Staff members often get used to the conditions without even noticing. This familiarity could cause additional issues for customer service.

SETTING THE STAGE

Assignment

Invite a consultant specializing in your type of operation or a manager from a similar operation to review your site and recommend new operational techniques or other suggestions for improvement. You will likely be surprised how helpful the "new set of eyes" will be on your operation.

Section II

Fostering Top-Rate Visitor Engagement

Because we enjoy working in nature and we see the visitors enjoying it as well, it is easy to rest on that observation and think our job is done. There is so much more to making a visitor experience complete. The entire operation's positive image and reputation are critical in attracting new visitors and retaining loyal ones.

Think about the influence certain positions within our operations have on visitors' impression formation. In some cases, they may have been imprinted on our visitors' imaginations since they were children. It is hard to accept, but in many cases, the positions we represent are sometimes almost as popular as the nature we are presenting. Through the years, we have heard so many visitors say, "I always wanted to be a Park Ranger." Wow, what a responsibility to maintain that image that so many created for us years before.

This section presents an array of helpful techniques that some might think are basic human relations and might be easily overlooked. As much as we think we do these, somehow, they are often not practiced to their fullest extent. We must always strive to refine both our verbal and non-verbal communications with a goal of truly connecting intellectually and emotionally with our visitors.

Genuine visitor engagement creates an atmosphere of acceptance that will build trust in our visitors and community. Our visitors crave the stories we are telling, and they want to not only hear them but feel them, see them, and fully experience them. This is best accomplished by providing innovative visitor engagement opportunities often through face-to-face encounters with authentic staff members.

As you review this section, think of other ways you and your team can create opportunities to foster top-rate visitor engagement within your operation.

1	2	3	4	5	6	7	8	9	10
11	12	13	14	15	16	17	18	19	20
21	22	**23**	**24**	**25**	**26**	**27**	**28**	**29**	**30**
31	**32**	**33**	**34**	**35**	**36**	**37**	**38**	**39**	**40**
41	**42**	**43**	**44**	**45**	46	47	48	49	50
51	52	53	54	55	56	57	58	59	60
61	62	63	64	65	66	67	68	69	70
71	72	73	74	75	76	77	78	79	80
81	82	83	84	85	86	87	88	89	90
91	92	93	94	95	96	97	98	99	100
101	102	103	104	105	106	107	108	109	110
111	112	113	114	115	116	117	118	119	120
121	122	123	124	125	126	127	128	129	130
131	132	133	134	135	136	137	138	139	140
141	142	143	144	145	146	147	148	149	150
151	152	153	154	155	156	157	158	159	160
161	162	163	164	165	166	167	168	169	170
171	172	173	174	175	176	177	178	179	180

Technique #23

Understand the Key Role of Face-to-Face Encounters

Research consistently demonstrates that visitors to ecotourism sites who have face-to-face interactions with staff members are typically more highly satisfied than those who do not have a staff interaction.[6] The authenticity of your operation is simply enhanced by interactions with friendly, knowledgeable, and competent staff.

VISITOR ENGAGEMENT

Assignment

For the primary purpose of visitor interaction, encourage your staff to regularly walk into heavily used areas and interact with the visitors. Even if some visitors will not get the pleasure of verbally communicating with your staff, they will likely benefit from the non-verbal communication associated with seeing them. Be prepared to receive appreciation as well as comments and suggestions.

Moreover, when your attraction is closed due to circumstances such as a natural disaster or pandemic, can technologies such as Zoom be employed to continue delivering such interactions?

Technique #24

Engrain the Drama Metaphor

All staff members should be taught that they are on-stage whenever a guest can see or hear them.[7] Therefore, on-stage behavior applies to all staff members regardless of whether or not they are clocked-in for work. That is, visitors perceive a uniformed employee as a representative of the attraction regardless of the circumstances.

> VISITOR ENGAGEMENT

Assignment

Train and remind staff that their image easily becomes the operation's image. Whether on or off duty, intended or not, their image reflects on the operation. Remind staff that the perception of the visitors is the reality of the situation, not the intent of staff. Therefore, positive personal behavior is expected.

Technique #25

Actively Communicate the "Must See"

At entrances, staff should ask visitors who they do not recognize if it is their first visit. If the answer is "yes" then the staff should communicate the must-see of the attraction. This tactic is important so that the site's most impressive feature(s) can help shape the impressions of the first-time visitors.

VISITOR ENGAGEMENT

Assignment

Create a one-on-one training program in which two staff members face each other and practice variations of this concept that are accepted by management and authentic to your area. This should be facilitated by someone with knowledge of the desired outcome.

Technique #26

Consider Adopting Real-Time Informational Capability

In recent years, IT products and services that can provide information to visitors (via their mobile devices) as they move through an attraction have both advanced in quality and reduced in price. Some of these technology products require internet connectivity which is also rapidly expanding into remote areas where many eco-sites are located, while others can be used with data alone. Such IT products can, for example, add more detail regarding context and history about a site that a visitor is viewing. A beneficial aspect associated with adopting these technologies is that visitors can decide for themselves whether or not to use them.

VISITOR ENGAGEMENT

Assignment

Research the products and IT service providers in your area. Ask ecotourism providers at other attractions currently using these products which ones they would recommend. Set-up 2-3 demos with selected vendors and involve staff members that interact with visitors the most. With IT service providers, fully understand who will manage the content.

Technique #27

Look Outside the Industry for Visitor Engagement Innovations

Ecotourism providers should exchange best practices with one another...however... often the most innovative ideas for visitor experience creation will derive from outside the industry. That is, it is often ideas being transplanted from other industries that spawn the most creative visitor engagement interactions: for example, ideas adopted from theme parks, movie theaters, shopping malls, hotels, etc.

> VISITOR ENGAGEMENT

Assignment

Discuss the following with the team: Outside of work, when they visit other service environments, what ideas do they witness that would be novel and innovative if applied to an ecotourism context? Your visitors demand the genuineness of your site and also really appreciate innovative visitor engagement.

Technique #28

Require One New Visitor Engagement Idea Per Week

Every week, one staff member should be required to share an innovative visitor engagement idea with the group that has never before been implemented at the ecotourism site. This "regular interval" requirement is useful so that multiple weeks do not pass during the site's busy season with no new innovation.

VISITOR ENGAGEMENT

Assignment

Team to discuss the logistics of this idea-sharing process. On which day will the idea be shared? Does the group have a weekly meeting or informal gathering? Change the interval if needed but this technique can motivate the team to always be innovative with visitor engagement. If weekly will not work in your operation, choose another time increment that suits your team.

Technique #29

Take Visitors' Photos

Staff members have unique opportunities to witness visitors enjoying the operations. When staff members see a group or family near a picture-worthy area, staff can offer to take a picture of them with their camera or phone. Some visitors may think that it could be a bother to ask you and they will be pleasantly surprised to be asked.

VISITOR ENGAGEMENT

Assignment

Gather your team and have everyone share their 3 favorite places in the operation to have their photos taken. Then encourage your staff to look for photo opportunities in these great locations. Your visitors will enjoy the photo and will remember that a staff member took it.

Technique #30

Acknowledge a Visitor Celebrating a Special Event

Each day, we meet many visitors at our operations. Some of these visitors are celebrating a special event in their lives. Staff recognizing these life events makes the visitors feel special and contributes to the overall positive memory of their visit. Just one staff member saying, "congratulations" can result in a future return visit.

VISITOR ENGAGEMENT

Assignment

At the next staff meeting, brainstorm how the details of this idea will work at your operation. An example would be that once a staff member finds out about the celebration, he or she quietly tells other staff members, so they can stop by and acknowledge them during their visit.

Technique #31

Reinforce the Importance of being Consistent with Terminology

Nomenclature used by staff should be consistent from all staff members as they communicate with visitors. If there is not a common name for one of your facilities, it may cause confusion among them. This can also cause possible catastrophic ramifications when responding to an emergency location that is not completely understood by everyone.

VISITOR ENGAGEMENT

Assignment

Give each of your staff members a short questionnaire to gauge consistency. What is the name of the first building that visitors come to? What is the name of the picnic area on the lake? What do we call the people that visit our park?

Technique #32

Engrain the Ten Foot Rule

During new staff orientation, it must be emphasized to all new hires that they must greet visitors whenever they pass within 10 feet of them. It is never acceptable to not greet a guest. If the guest is on his/her mobile phone then a smile, a nod, and a wave can serve as the greeting.

VISITOR ENGAGEMENT

Assignment

Team to discuss whether the 10-foot rule is currently covered in new staff orientation. If not, how can it be incorporated? If 10 feet will not work in your operation, choose another distance and an agreed upon minimum gesture.

Technique #33

Maintain Eye Contact

In many parts of the world, eye contact is a very powerful form of communication.[8] We should never miss the opportunity to make eye contact and say hello to the visitors in our operation. However, there are times when employees are so focused on their tasks, that they miss this opportunity.

> VISITOR ENGAGEMENT

Assignment

Maintaining eye contact may be more difficult for some staff members than for others. Create a safe environment for team members to practice this skill. Have staff members stand and face each other and practice speaking while making eye contact. This should be facilitated by someone with knowledge of the desired outcome.

Technique #34

Offer to Cover the Cost of Postage on Outbound Postcards

Offering free postage on visitors' outbound postcards will: 1) pleasantly surprise visitors; and 2) serve as low cost marketing for postcard recipients. If you are a government agency and this technique is not allowed, there are other ways to provide this service. Think about how your community can participate in this effort. For instance, maybe free postage could be available at the local welcome center, restaurant, or other community partner.

VISITOR ENGAGEMENT

Assignment

Discuss the following with the team: 1) Does your current selection of postcards represent your attraction in the best possible light? 2) How would the offer to cover the cost of postage be communicated to visitors? Work with the community to help provide this service.

Technique #35

Post a Daily Weather Forecast

When visitors to your operation are traveling for more than a few days, quite often they are not following the weather forecast for your specific location. Many of your visitors are familiar with their local weather patterns and meteorological signs but when traveling, they may not track or understand your local weather.

VISITOR ENGAGEMENT

Assignment

Every morning, print the local weather forecast from a trusted website and post it on counters, doors, or other common areas within your operation. Your visitors will thank you for helping them stay safe and preparing them for their day of adventure.

Technique #36

Have Commonly Forgotten Items Available

Campers generally have more to pack, transport, and set-up than most of your visitors. There is a good chance, at some point in their travels, they will forget something. The feeling of forgetting something can be nerve rattling. Therefore, the fact that an item has been forgotten can be a hindrance to their positive experience.

VISITOR ENGAGEMENT

Assignment

Provide for sale or direct them outside your operation, common items that campers forget. Ask your staff to brainstorm the top 3 items campers forget to pack. Charcoal, firewood, tent stakes, tarpaulins, water supply hoses, electric hookup adapters and insect repellents may be on the list. Commonly forgotten items that are inexpensive, such as toothpaste, can be offered for free.

Technique #37

Remember Names and Train the 'Again' Effect

During new staff orientation, everyone should be provided with some tactics regarding how to remember repeat visitors' names.[9]

Because some ecotourism sites receive high volumes of visitors, it is not possible to remember all frequent visitors' names. Therefore, if a staff member recognizes a visitor as being a repeat patron, but cannot recall his/her name, the staff member should be trained to say, 'nice to see you again.' Inserting the word 'again' helps strengthen the relationship between the visitor and provider.

VISITOR ENGAGEMENT

Assignment

Discuss as a team how many names of regular visitors each person on the team knows. Brainstorm strategies for learning more names. Train staff to have a response when they recognize someone but cannot recall their name. This response should not sound forced or contrived and should be authentic to the community you represent.

Technique #38

Thank Visitors for Constructive Feedback

If a visitor has a valid concern, it is better that s/he communicates it directly to the provider rather than spreading negative word of mouth or not returning. Therefore, staff should be trained to thank guests for sharing their constructive feedback directly with a member of the team.[10]

VISITOR ENGAGEMENT

Assignment

Discuss as a team what systems are in place to properly handle constructive feedback and valid complaints. How can these systems be improved? Train staff to openly accept possible criticism about the operation and to respond by showing appreciation for sharing this constructive feedback.

Technique #39

Interact with Strength on the Telephone

Often, when a potential visitor telephones the attraction, this is the first (and could be the last) human interaction that s/he is having with the staff. As such, all staff should:

- State their names when they answer a call
- Thank the caller
- Smile when on the telephone (because smiling changes voice inflection; callers can tell)
- Invite the caller to visit

VISITOR ENGAGEMENT

Assignment

What training systems does the team have in place to ensure that telephone interactions are handled with the attention that they deserve? Perhaps let staff stand and face each other and have them take turns pretending to answer the phone. In this role playing, encourage the other staff members to ask common questions. This should be facilitated by someone with knowledge of the desired outcome.

Technique #40

Afford Special Attention to Children

Children visiting the ecotourism site should be positively surprised through the use of inexpensive / free interaction-based tactics.[11] Options might include Park Ranger stickers, selecting a gift from a treasure chest, solving a riddle, engaging in a scavenger hunt, etc. Create a memory for them and one day they will return with their children.

VISITOR ENGAGEMENT

Assignment

Team to brainstorm creative ways to positively surprise children. Because (by definition) someone can only be surprised by something one time, a variety of surprise tactics should be adopted. Try to relate the engagement to the theme of your site. Have fun and let your inner child come out.

Technique #41

Use Welcoming Verbal and Non-Verbal Cues

When a visitor asks a staff member "How are you?", responses such as "good, because it is almost 5:00" or "good, because I am off tomorrow" do not engender a welcoming atmosphere. Likewise, when a visitor says "thank you", a strong response is needed. For instance, staff can be taught to reply with "thank you" when a guest says, "thank you". Replies to "thank you" such as "no problem" do not communicate appreciation or leave a lasting impression.

Regarding non-verbal cues, the most welcoming gesture is a smile which communicates to the visitor: "I am glad that you are here right now."[12]

VISITOR ENGAGEMENT

Assignment

How can the team be more aware of the conscious and subconscious signals that they communicate to visitors through their verbal and non-verbal cues? Engage staff members to derive acceptable responses. Sometimes, the acceptable responses might sound corny because they are not trendy. But a response, said sincerely, will be welcomed by your visitors.

Technique #42

Invite First Time Visitors to Identify Themselves

Ecotourism sites should consider posting a message such as "If You Are Visiting for the First Time, Please See a Member of Our Staff for a Token of Our Appreciation." The logic here is to encourage visitor-staff interaction, so that first time visitors can be transformed into loyal patrons and advocates. Out of practicality, it might only be possible to display such a message on days when the attraction is experiencing low visitor volumes.

VISITOR ENGAGEMENT

Assignment

Discuss with the team what is currently being done to recognize and formulate relationships with first time patrons. How can these practices be improved? Maybe there is not an actual token but simply the opportunity to interact with a staff member.

Technique #43

Circumvent Awkward Silence

There are times when a staff member will be registering a visitor for entrance, lodging, or an activity and the computer's operating system is running slow or other technical issues transpire. This situation often makes the staff member feel uncomfortable because the visitor is looking at them while the staff member is looking at the computer monitor.

VISITOR ENGAGEMENT

Assignment

Train all staff members that could find themselves in this situation not to speak poorly about the technical situation. Instead, use this time to ask a question to the visitor. Examples can be: "how was your drive here?" or "where are you visiting us from?"

Technique #44

Anticipate Visitors' Questions About the Local Area

There are times when staff may be asked to provide a recommendation on local businesses. As part of their overall stay in the area, visitors may need camping supplies, internet access, or medical care. Some government operated sites do not allow a staff member to recommend a particular establishment but will allow staff to provide helpful information.

VISITOR ENGAGEMENT

Assignment

At your regularly scheduled staff meeting, incorporate a quiz to help your employees remember which businesses provide what services or supplies. Examples: what stores sell ice? what stores sell firewood? what stores sell sunscreen? what store has a late hour pharmacy? Where are the nearest urgent care facilities?

Technique #45

Properly Thank Visitors

Visitors have almost limitless options of where to spend their discretionary time and money. They did not need to select your attraction. In fact, they may have passed up other sites on the way to yours. Therefore, all staff members should be trained to thank them for their patronage. Thanking visitors communicates appreciation.

VISITOR ENGAGEMENT

Assignment

What training systems does the team have in place to ensure that visitors are properly thanked and that strong verbal communication practices are in place? Training and follow-up with all staff members can really make a difference. Try to catch each other saying thank you and compliment each other to other staff members.

Section III

Recruiting, Selecting, and Motivating Your Team

Each day we present the authentic and genuine natural and cultural resources that our sites possess. It is likely not a coincidence that many of our staff members are cut from the same cloth, authentic and genuine. In many operations, the resources and staff members complement each other and seem to fit seamlessly into the overall theme of the site.

Recruiting, interviewing, onboarding, training, and motivating staff members is an expensive investment in both time and money… but… it is more expensive not to do these things correctly. Extensive follow up, performance problems, and discipline become an issue and can be emotionally draining on staff and will most likely affect your customer relations.

Many operations have seasonal peaks and valleys that require staff members to have flexible hours or certain times of year when needed. Seasonal and part time employees often make up the greatest number of staff members but often receive the least amount of training and coaching. These individuals will often fill full time core positions as they become available. Special attention needs to be afforded to make sure they receive all the tools they need to perform their roles.

In some cases, we do not have total control over the human resources procedures that we are required to follow, but we all have an important role in the overall cohesiveness of the team. Coaching between coworkers by encouraging and supporting each other can be a powerful teambuilding tool that can be fostered through time.

Exceptional organizations actively manage the entire human resources process, continuously adapting different strategies to help their employees achieve greatness. This section offers techniques that can be helpful for you and your team to do just that. Each one of them can be slightly modified to fit into the culture of your operation or can be used as presented.

1	2	3	4	5	6	7	8	9	10
11	12	13	14	15	16	17	18	19	20
21	22	23	24	25	26	27	28	29	30
31	32	33	34	35	36	37	38	39	40
41	42	43	44	45	**46**	**47**	**48**	**49**	**50**
51	**52**	**53**	**54**	**55**	**56**	**57**	**58**	**59**	**60**
61	**62**	**63**	**64**	**65**	**66**	**67**	**68**	69	70
71	72	73	74	75	76	77	78	79	80
81	82	83	84	85	86	87	88	89	90
91	92	93	94	95	96	97	98	99	100
101	102	103	104	105	106	107	108	109	110
111	112	113	114	115	116	117	118	119	120
121	122	123	124	125	126	127	128	129	130
131	132	133	134	135	136	137	138	139	140
141	142	143	144	145	146	147	148	149	150
151	152	153	154	155	156	157	158	159	160
161	162	163	164	165	166	167	168	169	170
171	172	173	174	175	176	177	178	179	180

Technique #46

Write Realistic, Yet Creative, Job Announcements

In our industry, potential applicants may have an unrealistic or romantic idea of the real duties for a staff position. For instance, some may think that River Guides just float down the river and Park Naturalists only deliver interpretive programs. A realistic job announcement describing even the non-glamorous duties may reduce the size of the applicant pool but may also increase the overall understanding and commitment required.

With the above stated, any accolades, bragging-points, or unique features of your site that would inspire someone to desire to be part of the team should be included in the announcement.[13]

STAFF PERFORMANCE

Assignment

Rewrite 3 of your most frequently available positions. Ask the current incumbents of these positions to describe a difficult day and consider using that information in your rewrite. In addition, what are some justifiable reasons why someone might want to join the team? How can this information be incorporated as well?

Technique #47

Aid Staff Recruitment by Showing Off Your Winning Team

Future staff members want to be a part of a winning team. Take advantage of every opportunity in your community to highlight your winning operation at community gatherings and events. Current staff members will have a sense of pride participating in these events and will display their passion they have for your operation.

> STAFF PERFORMANCE

Assignment

Commit to participating in an event each quarter. Suggested events include job fairs, career days, community events, parades, etc. Reach out to the communities within an hour's drive of your site for these opportunities. Select staff members who are passionate about your operation to participate.

Technique #48

Conduct Multiple Day Interviewing When Possible

Sub-optimal visitor experiences are more likely to transpire when the attraction is understaffed due to staff tardiness or a no-show. Consequently, whenever possible, applicants for staff positions should be asked to return for interviews on more than one day in order to gauge their dependability and demeanor at various points in time.

STAFF PERFORMANCE

Assignment

Supervisory staff to discuss whether multiple day interviews are currently being used. If not, can they be incorporated when filling certain positions? The first interview could be in the morning and might include technical questions. The second interview could be in the afternoon on another day and could include a discussion about the mission of your operation.

Technique #49

Screen for Emotional Intelligence in the Interview

Often, especially in large or remote operations, staff members work away from a fellow staff member or a supervisor. These assignments may include giving a program in town, leading a group down river, or mending a fence in a remote location. These assignments often involve significant situational awareness and the emotional intelligence of these employees must be high.[14]

STAFF PERFORMANCE

Assignment

Add 3 additional interview questions to help you identify the emotional intelligence of the applicants. Ask questions to understand the applicants' values, what inspires them, and their acceptance of constructive criticism. Present a scenario and ask: what would you do? How would that make you feel? Tell me the best options for resolution?

Technique #50

Test a Job Applicant's Ability to Get to the Facts

The ability of our staff to correctly document an incident continues to be an important aspect of many of our positions. Report writing skills need to be sharp and the report not only needs to have accurate information but understandable to anyone outside of your operation. Just the facts without judgement, assumptions, or hearsay is usually the best course to take.

STAFF PERFORMANCE

Assignment

Choose a news story video of an incident or a scene in a movie and show it to an applicant during the interview. Provide access to a computer and ask him/her to draft a document describing the incident. The results will help you determine many attributes of the applicant.

Technique #51

Assess the Applicant's Conversational Ability

Staff members need to possess the ability to have meaningful and genuine conversations with visitors. Such conversational ability can be assessed during the interview by asking creative questions to which answers cannot be pre-scripted. A panel-style interview in which the applicant is simultaneously interviewed by more than one individual is another means of gauging an applicant's conversational ability.[15]

STAFF PERFORMANCE

Assignment

What methods do you have in place for assessing applicants' conversational ability? How can these methods be improved? Still using your time-tested interview questions but after the applicant answers them once, ask for additional answers. This would frustrate some but those with conversational ability will shine.

Technique #52

Increase the Likelihood that the Top Candidate Will Accept the Position

When interviewing a job candidate, if the interviewer is pleased with the performance of the candidate, the interviewer should make a point of telling the applicant about some of the accolades secured by the attraction and/or some of the unique selling points of the attraction. Share information about the great staff and that they would be a part of the winning team.[16]

> STAFF PERFORMANCE

Assignment

Supervisory staff to discuss whether or not the top candidates have accepted offers when they have been extended. If not, what are some measures that can be taken to improve the success rate in recruiting the best possible staff?

Technique #53

Harness Economic Impacts as a Contributor of Pride

As will be explained later in this Handbook, it is recommended that the attraction calculate economic impacts on an annual basis. Such economic impact metrics might include jobs supported, labor income, tax revenue generation, and contributions to the gross domestic product (GDP).

The entire team should know the attraction's economic impacts because 1) they can communicate those impacts; and 2) the impacts contribute to a sense of pride as the figures reinforce the importance of their work.

STAFF PERFORMANCE

Assignment

Once annual economic impact reports are published, the team should be trained on how to interpret and communicate them. If calculating economic impacts is not a skill included in your current staff portfolio, consider investing in a service that specializes in these important analyses.

Technique #54

Provide Business Cards to All Staff Members

Business cards for all your employees is an easy way to show professionalism within your operation. These inexpensive cards can be given to visitors as a part of many interactions with staff. The visitor will be impressed by the thoughtfulness and professionalism. Moreover, your staff will feel a sense of pride making the cards available.

STAFF PERFORMANCE

Assignment

Design business cards with all the pertinent information about your operation but not the staff member. Create a line on the card so every staff member can handwrite their name for a personal touch. Key staff members should have their own customized cards.

Technique #55

Empower Staff Members Through Delegation

Our staff members have their regular job duties that they enjoy and are proficient at. A good way to keep them motivated is to delegate a task or project that is not a part of their regular assigned tasks but is within their capabilities. This delegation can be motivational if learning the new task is perceived by the staff member as a boundary-spanning way to advance his/her knowledge and career competencies.[17]

STAFF PERFORMANCE

Assignment

Select a task or project that you want accomplished and a staff member who you believe has the knowledge, skills, and abilities to succeed. The task or project should be challenging but not overwhelming. Consider something small at first then slowly increase the complexity and importance in concert with career progression.

Technique #56

Motivate with Mirrors

Our uniform is a great way by which we are identified by our visitors. It provides a sense of authority and comfort that the operation is run by professionals. The uniform also gives staff members a sense of pride as they represent the operation. Uniforms standards should be created to complement the operation's mission and theme.

> STAFF PERFORMANCE

Assignment

By the nature of our work in rugged environmental conditions, staff appearance can easily become disheveled if we do not give our appearance the attention it deserves. Place full-length mirrors in several strategic locations within your operation so that staff members see themselves as they pass by. The self-views reflected in the mirrors will serve as reminders and motivators regarding the importance of attention to detail in appearance.

Technique #57

Print Hometowns on Nametags

All team members should have their hometowns printed on their nametags. This practice is motivating for the team member because it signals to him/her that s/he is valued and not just a name. Moreover, this practice can, in many cases, serve as a conversational ice breaker between the visitor and staff member.

STAFF PERFORMANCE

Assignment

Discuss with your team the logistics of printing hometowns on name tags. Who will spearhead the initiative? What will be the implementation timeline? If this is not feasible on name tags, consider printing desk name plates with hometowns on them. This works out well when a staff member is designated to a counter-type assignment.

Technique #58

Recognize Staff for Exceptional Failure Recovery Efforts

Visitors in service environments such as ecotourism sites have heightened attention when something goes wrong.[18] Therefore, if a staff member goes the extra-mile to solve a visitor's problem or handle a problematic situation, it is a big deal. Particular attention should be given to situations in which the staff member offered aid/comfort to problems not caused by the organization: e.g. a visitor locking the keys inside his/her car.

STAFF PERFORMANCE

Assignment

Team to discuss how such a failure recovery recognition system should be designed. As an example, take a digital photo of the staff member and write a few sentence narrative about what s/he did in the situation. Publicize this photo and narrative within your organization.

Technique #59

Convene Staff Meetings At Least Once Per Month

Communication is a two-way street that fosters trust with staff members. Not surprisingly, communication and trust are highly correlated with motivation and performance. However, many times our operations seem to be moving so fast that there is only time for one-sided communication such as emails and directives.

STAFF PERFORMANCE

Assignment

Hold a formal or informal meeting once a month at a time and day that most staff can attend. The agenda could include a financial overview, operation safety, or what flower is blooming in the meadow. Ensure everyone has the opportunity to share their thoughts during the meeting.

Technique #60

Require Visitor Encounter Stories During Staff Meetings

During a staff meeting, each person in the meeting should be asked to state something about one visitor that they met since the previous meeting. Examples could include the visitor's name; the place of residency of the visitor; the reason for the visitor being in the area; or, other destinations visited on the same trip. This practice of recounting visitor-related information will help motivate the staff to interact with visitors.

STAFF PERFORMANCE

Assignment

Decide whether this practice will take place at the beginning of the meeting or the end. Give staff warning that this practice is coming so that they are not unprepared / embarrassed in front of the team. There is no right or wrong with staff's stories, just that they participate.

Technique #61

Require One Visitor Surprise Story During Staff Meetings

During the staff meeting, one staff member should be randomly selected to describe a creative situation in which s/he surprised a visitor in a positive way since the last meeting. This practice will help reinforce the notion of surprising visitors with small gestures of kindness. This can be fun for both visitors and staff members.

STAFF PERFORMANCE

Assignment

Notify the team that this practice is coming and why. When implemented, one method of random selection is to write the word "yes" on a sticky note and leave all the others blank. The staff member who draws the "yes" sheet tells the story.

Technique #62

Always Wish Happy Holidays

In our industry, operations are often open 24/7 throughout the year. Often, less seasoned staff are assigned to work during these shifts while senior leadership positions have the day off. This can create a challenge for leadership to truly show their appreciation to all employees especially to the ones working on holidays.

STAFF PERFORMANCE

Assignment

During a holiday, have leadership staff contact their direct reports who are working each shift. Stop by in person, call on the phone, or radio them. Let them know how much you appreciate them and how much their service means to the visitors. Wish them a happy holiday.

Technique #63

Set Team Goals

Set team goals on which progress can be monitored. Goals are important because most humans have an inherent desire to achieve something. Making progress towards goals feels good for everyone on the team... if... everyone on the team understands why attaining the goals is important.[19]

STAFF PERFORMANCE

Assignment

What goals will your team set for the upcoming season? Setting goals requires a lot of thought: goals that are attained too easily are not necessarily motivating; conversely, unattainable goals are also not motivational. What can be done so that the team understands the importance of the goals? For instance, should the goals be collaboratively set by the team?

Technique #64

Provide Feedback Everyday

If you see someone on your team doing something well: tell him/her that s/he is doing it well. If you see someone on your team doing something that can be improved: give him/her constructive feedback. Humans love feedback and, in many cases, even constructive feedback is more motivational than no feedback at all.

A regular stream of feedback will keep your good staff members on your team; conversely, if bad habits permeate the team due to lack of feedback, the good staff members are more apt to pursue other opportunities outside of your organization.

> STAFF PERFORMANCE

Assignment

How much feedback is being provided to the staff members? Not at the individual-level, but rather at the team-level, positive feedback should always be more common than constructive feedback. If constructive feedback represents the majority, then a 'nitpicky' culture might be perceived. On the other hand, if positive feedback is the majority, then a positive vibe will emerge.

Technique #65

Have Creative, Yet Fair, Recognition Programs

Design staff recognition programs that are creative, but the programs should give all staff members equal likelihood of winning. For example, a team reward such as a pizza party can be administered when the site's guest satisfaction survey score targets are met or exceeded. Gift cards to area stores and restaurants also seem to be a well-received prize.

STAFF PERFORMANCE

Assignment

Using input from all, design a recognition program that is creative, fun, and fair. Because it's the staff's reward, try your best to accommodate their suggestions as outlandish as they might be. Ask businesses and other partners in the community to participate in this recognition.

Technique #66

Include Customer Service Performance in Staff Evaluations

The standard form on which to complete all staff members' written performance evaluations should contain a section evaluating customer service. For non-customer contact staff, items such as teamwork and dependability can be addressed in this section because these items impact visitor satisfaction perceptions.

STAFF PERFORMANCE

Assignment

Team to discuss how customer service performance can be further incorporated into the evaluation process. If a government entity, what procedures need to be followed to amend the performance evaluation criteria to include customer service?

Technique #67

Don't Drop the Ball with Seasonal Staff

Visitors should receive the same level of friendliness, engagement, and professionalism from seasonal staff that they receive from the site's permanent staff. In the eyes of visitors, all are equally representing the brand. Recruitment, training, expectation, appearance, and behavior-standards are just a few telltale elements of a united staff.

STAFF PERFORMANCE

Assignment

Team to discuss methods to ensure that seasonal staff members are a seamless representation of your attraction. For instance, is there an on-boarding or orientation process for these individuals? Create or enhance the orientation program of these important team members.

Technique #68

Use Uniforms to Help Unify

The only people that should know whether a staff member is seasonal, part time, or part of the core staff should be the staff, not the visitor. Visitors desire quality experiences and interactions regardless of who on the team they are interacting with. As such, uniforms are a time-tested way to present a unifying image to your visitors. Uniforms help reinforce consistency both on a conscious and sub-conscious level from both the visitors' point of view and among the staff members themselves.

STAFF PERFORMANCE

Assignment

Take photos of a core staff member next to a part time and seasonal staff member. Will a visitor to your operation know the difference? If so, do you want that image differentiated? How does that help or hurt the visitor's impression of the operation? If a modification in uniform is decided upon, a professional uniform provider can help you create the uniform image right for your operation.

Section IV

Attracting Visitors to Your Site

Today's visitors have many day-to-day distractions. The world is more mechanized and has more comforts than ever before. We live by the calendar and time constraints and it seems like there is always one more thing to do. When our visitors carve-out some time to get outside to enjoy nature or their community, there is a lot of competition for their time. Events, festivals, and one-of-a-kind experiences await them.

Positioning an operation to achieve the greatest exposure takes expertise, patience and yes... some trial and error. You may be wondering... Which marketing platforms should we use? What aspect of our services should we market? Who should we target with our marketing? And many more questions including how are we going to pay for it? And how can we determine our return on investment (ROI)?

With increasing competition on people's free time from our competitors, the question is not if we should market our site but how to market our site. If this is not your area of expertise, perhaps a staff member or vendor can provide guidance. Luckily, there are many experts we can rely on and many free or less expensive platforms to consider. A solid plan will help our team keep focused on the prize.

Employing marketing research, visitor satisfaction surveys, website / social media analytics, and other tools will help with data driven decisions. However, marketing is as much as an art form as it is a science, so commonsense and trusting our instincts are definitely parts of the equation.

As you review this section, think of other ways you and your team can attract visitors to your operation.

1	2	3	4	5	6	7	8	9	10
11	12	13	14	15	16	17	18	19	20
21	22	23	24	25	26	27	28	29	30
31	32	33	34	35	36	37	38	39	40
41	42	43	44	45	46	47	48	49	50
51	52	53	54	55	56	57	58	59	60
61	62	63	64	65	66	67	68	**69**	**70**
71	**72**	**73**	**74**	**75**	**76**	**77**	**78**	**79**	**80**
81	**82**	**83**	**84**	**85**	**86**	**87**	**88**	**89**	**90**
91	92	93	94	95	96	97	98	99	100
101	102	103	104	105	106	107	108	109	110
111	112	113	114	115	116	117	118	119	120
121	122	123	124	125	126	127	128	129	130
131	132	133	134	135	136	137	138	139	140
141	142	143	144	145	146	147	148	149	150
151	152	153	154	155	156	157	158	159	160
161	162	163	164	165	166	167	168	169	170
171	172	173	174	175	176	177	178	179	180

Technique #69

Understand the Leading Way to Attract Visitors

When visitors are asked on surveys which information sources they used when deciding to visit, the two information sources that most frequently emerge at the top of the list are:
1. Memories of past trips
2. Word-of-mouth

The above two information sources typically trump all other information channels: road signs, social media, newspaper / magazine coverage, etc.

ATTRACTING VISITORS

Assignment

Be sure that your team knows that the leading way to attract more visitors is to deliver exceptional experiences to the ones that are there. In other words, the top marketing tool is experience delivery. This should be communicated on a routine basis to staff to reinforce the importance of top-rate visitor engagement.

Technique #70

Post Short Videos on Facebook

Post short videos (one minute or less) on Facebook featuring your offerings. These videos should be enjoyable for viewing with or without audio. If possible, these videos should incorporate drone footage of your attraction. The production should have a good balance of scenic vistas and visitors recreating and enjoying themselves.[20]

ATTRACTING VISITORS

Assignment

Discuss with your team what should be filmed and who will serve as the videographer. A good eye and a steady hand are desired traits. Consult with your attorney if "model releases" are required in your area before filming.

Technique #71

Experiment with Twitter and Instagram

The word "experiment" is purposefully used because Twitter and Instagram communications have mixed results for ecotourism-related venues. Nevertheless, because of the low cost of pursuing this strategy, they are social media channels that can be tested. These platforms can be successful in creating awareness of your offerings.[21]

ATTRACTING VISITORS

Assignment

Discuss who on your team has experience with either Twitter or Instagram. What marketing messages should be sent through these channels? What stories do you want to tell? What products and services do you want to highlight? What does success look like? Create a plan and monitor your results.

Technique #72

Hone the Timing of Social Media Communications

When communications are sent across each of your social media channels, monitor **re**sponse to the messages relative to the time of day that the communication was sent. **By** monitoring and recording responses relative to time of day, social media strategies can **be** honed to maximize exposure/response.

ATTRACTING VISITORS

Assignment

Discuss who on your team will monitor social media back-end analytics to track effectiveness of timing strategies. Articulate the goals and define what success will look like for this initiative. Be flexible, creative, and relevant to the audience.

Technique #73

Harness the Power of Opt-In Email Marketing

Develop an email marketing list in which visitors who opt-in can receive special offers for dates/times when your attraction typically has large amounts of excess carrying capacity. It can also be used to promote special events, a unique live stream from your site, and/or seasonal offerings. For example, use it to spread the news about the recent baby animal born to create excitement.

ATTRACTING VISITORS

Assignment

Derive a plan among the team regarding how the email addresses will be gathered and who will be charged with designing and delivering the communications. Consider working with an IT vendor that can offer the latest innovation to reach your goals.

Technique #74

Periodically Use Sensory Messaging

In approximately 2 out of 3 visiting groups to ecotourism sites, a female is the primary decision maker in the group. Research indicates that sensory messaging – defined as messaging that describes the touch or smell of something – is one of the few types of marketing messaging that increases female appeal without hindering male appeal.[22]

ATTRACTING VISITORS

Assignment

Discuss with your team what sort of sensory messaging can be employed at your attraction: for example, "feel the sugary soft sand on your toes;" "enjoy the fragrance of the flowers in the meadow". Brainstorming will likely yield more sensory messaging ideas than anticipated.

Technique #75

Encourage Visitors to Blog About Their Positive Experiences

Visitors who are witnessed having positive experiences should be encouraged to blog about their experiences on TripAdvisor. This is important because TripAdvisor is king: experiencing about 400 million unique site visitors every month and about 300 reviews are posted on the site every minute.[23]

ATTRACTING VISITORS

Assignment

Team to develop a plan to encourage positive TripAdvisor reviews. The plan could include actions such as training staff regarding how to explain the procedures to visitors. Distributing business card-sized hand-outs with instructions and encouraging individuals to blog about their positive experiences.

Technique #76

Provide Familiarization (FAM) Visits to Local Hotel Staff

Local hotel staff would typically be more likely to recommend the ecotourism attraction if they have been there, met the team, and experienced the offerings. As such, local hotel staff should be invited to the attraction and provided with a complimentary or at-cost tour and use of the amenities.

ATTRACTING VISITORS

Assignment

Team to identify target hotels and a plan for arranging FAM visits. These can be scheduled once a month, once a quarter, or at a time when leadership staff are prepared to welcome them. Invite them to bring their families with them to create lasting memories.

Technique #77

Post Strong Responses to TripAdvisor Reviews

Post responses in TripAdvisor to both positive and negative reviews of your attraction. Responses should occur within seven days of the visitor's review.

- Responses to positive reviews should incorporate the name of your attraction and responses to negative posts should not.

- When responding to a negative online review, the responder should use 'I' in the online response (e.g. 'I will look into this issue'). The use of the word "I" signals ownership of the problem and resolution. On the other hand, when responding to a positive online review, the responder should use 'we' to spread the credit among the staff (e.g. 'we are very glad that you enjoyed your stay').[24]

ATTRACTING VISITORS

Assignment

Team to review the attraction's current TripAdvisor presence. How can this presence be improved? Consider assigning a specific staff member to monitor all responses. Have him/her "log in" and establish the "respond by" date so nothing is dropped.

Technique #78

Ensure the Accuracy of the Attraction's Wikipedia Page

Many parks, preserves, and nature-based historical sites have Wikipedia pages. It is important to check these Wikipedia pages for completeness and accuracy. These pages foster the visibility of the attraction. For instance, the more informed a Wikipedia page, the more likely a student will reference the page when conducting research for a term paper.

ATTRACTING VISITORS

Assignment

Team should review the site's Wikipedia presence and add / update information if needed. Consider assigning a specific staff member to monitor Wikipedia and make corrections as needed and add updates on a regular schedule.

Technique #79

Enhance Search Engine Optimization by Routinely Updating the Attraction's Website

Updates to the attraction's website will not only keep the information current and relevant but will also aid with search engine optimization (SEO). While algorithms that guide search engine retrieval continually change, one variable that is typically included in these algorithms is the recency of fresh content on websites.

ATTRACTING VISITORS

Assignment

The team should review the attraction website for accuracy and derive a plan for regular updates. Perhaps assign a specific staff member to monitor your website and add updates on a regular schedule. Or consider an IT vendor that provides these services.

Technique #80

Post Aerial Drone Footage on the Attraction's Website

While ecotourism sites exist in many forms, one thing that most have in common is that aerial video footage of the attraction can be quite magnificent. The recent advances in drone technology, coupled with price reductions, deem it increasingly possible to record high quality aerial footage of ecotourism attractions. Such footage can serve as a conduit for visitor awareness if posted on the attraction's website.

ATTRACTING VISITORS

Assignment

Does your team have access to a drone? Does your team know someone who is willing to record the footage on a pro-bono basis? Or consider hiring a professional drone pilot videographer. Either way, make sure s/he is a Certified Drone Pilot by the FAA. Go to FAA.com for more information. Some animals can be negatively impacted by drones; therefore, a knowledgeable staff member should be assigned to accompany the drone operator.

Technique #81

Host Travel Writers

Attractions possessing unique recreational, ecological, cultural, or historical characteristics are typically of interest to travel writers. Coverage by travel writers in print media and/or online outlets can be a significant influencer in potential visitors' decision-making. They are usually looking for locations and stories that they can get the "scoop" on that other writers have not written about.

ATTRACTING VISITORS

Assignment

Compile a list of travel writers to target for coverage and work through the list extending them invitations for familiarization (FAM) visits. Articulate how your operation is unique in your offerings. Ask them what they are interested in writing about and try to meet or exceed their requirements.

Technique #82

Organize a Photo Contest

While nature-based destinations exist in many forms, one thing that they all have in common is natural beauty. Photo contests in which visitors submit their pictures can be very effective in not only further engaging with current patrons but also in creating buzz on social media. What a great opportunity for your community to participate in as well.

ATTRACTING VISITORS

Assignment

Discuss with your team how the photo contest will be publicized, the parameters of the contest, the prize, and other details. Design the contest so you have the photographer's permission to use the submitted photos in both the present and future.

Technique #83

Send Feel-Good News to the Media

When events that impact the attraction and/or surrounding community in a positive way such as charity fundraisers, scout projects, garden club events, etc. are held on-site, announcements should be sent to the media. Heart-warming stories are often afforded coverage in media outlets.

ATTRACTING VISITORS

Assignment

Determine if the team has a comprehensive and up-to-date list of local media contacts. If not, who will expand and up-date the list? Who on the team is responsible for serving as the media liaison? Most groups will welcome the media exposure but make sure they are asked in advance.

Technique #84

Publicize a January 1st Event

Few would refute that visiting a natural setting is a great way to begin a new year. Consider publicizing a January 1st event in which individuals can do just that. Something physical may check a box for those with the New Year's Resolution of losing weight or to get in shape. Often, local residents have visiting family and friends and are looking for something to do as a group.

ATTRACTING VISITORS

Assignment

Assign the planning and coordination of the January 1st event to a member of the team. Get input from staff on a fun activity that most visitors can participate in. For example, a "First Sunrise (or) Sunset Of The Year", "New Year's Day Polar Plunge Swimming Event" or "First Day Of The Year Walk Around The Lake Event."

Technique #85

Brag about Accolades

While this technique runs counter to our instinct to be humble, the concept of social proof contends that individuals both knowingly and unknowingly look to others when deciding on their own actions.[25] Therefore, publicizing a top TripAdvisor rating or a top REI hike rating will pull weight in attracting visitors.

ATTRACTING VISITORS

Assignment

Discuss with your team what accolade(s) your attraction has secured that can be more broadly communicated. In which channels should it be communicated? What other accolades can be pursued? Explore the processes to publicize the accolades on social media visitor experience/recommendation sites and apps.

Technique #86

Market for Slow Periods

Some attractions invest in marketing media to encourage visitation during a timeframe that is going to be at or near maximum capacity without the marketing. Whereas, to better balance supply and demand relationships, what is really needed is to market traditionally slow periods: e.g. Mondays during the shoulder season.

ATTRACTING VISITORS

Assignment

Before deciding upon marketing-related expenditures, always ask this question: Will the marketing initiative attract visitation during our typically slow periods? For attractions with multiple locations, such as national and state park systems, a related question should be asked: What marketing can be conducted to attract visitation to our less visited sites?

Technique #87

Post about Unique Natural Occurrences on Social Media

You may also consider live streaming certain natural occurrences if such streaming can be arranged safely, ethically, and without disturbing any wildlife/ecosystem involved.

The formation of unique ice crystals on trees, the hatching of sea turtles, the companionship between two park animals that typically are not thought of as companions, etc. Every ecotourism site should, at a minimum, have 5-6 unique natural occurrences per year that should be posted about on social media. There is a good likelihood of such posts going viral reminding past visitors to return and reaching other audiences who have never visited.

ATTRACTING VISITORS

Assignment

Discuss with the team your site's social media strategy. Do any measures need to be taken to make this strategy more consistent or proactive? List all the known unique natural occurrences within your operation and the time of years they occur. Create a timeline of when to post each occurrence and be careful to try to spread them throughout the year.

Technique #88

> **Verify whether the Brand's Tagline Adequately Differentiates the Attraction(s)**

If a branding tagline is generic and could describe any ecotourism destination, then it is probably not pulling its weight in helping to attract visitors. In the assessment of the authors of this book, the following are well-crafted taglines:

Virginia State Parks: "I Love Virginia State Parks." ^{SM}

This is a differentiating brand because it connects the park system to the state's umbrella brand: "Virginia is for Lovers" which is the longest running statewide tourism brand in the U.S.

Saugatuck / Douglas, Michigan: "The Art Coast of Michigan." ^{SM}

This is a differentiating brand because the two common themes that drive visitation are the beaches / waters on Lake Michigan and the arts (art in many forms: visual arts, performing arts, culinary arts, etc).

> ATTRACTING VISITORS

Assignment

Discuss whether your brand adequately differentiates your attraction. What has happened within your operation since the tagline was written? How has your community changed? In what direction are your visitors leaning? Are there new competitors? There are many areas to consider and a consultant can help guide this process.

Technique #89

Administer a Marketing ROI Survey

Visitors should periodically be encouraged to complete a brief online survey that gathers data such as what information source(s) they used when deciding to visit, how far in advance they made the decision to visit, and which other destinations they visited during the same trip. This information will aid in maximizing the return on investment (ROI) of marketing expenditures.

ATTRACTING VISITORS

Assignment

Craft a survey internally or contact a local university or consulting practice for guidance developing / implementing the survey. Understand the science and art of carefully written questions to draw-out the information you need to inform your strategies.

Technique #90

Conduct Web Analytics

Incorporate your web address in as many of your marketing efforts as possible. Monitor analytics surrounding your web traffic such as:

- Geographic origin of website traffic
- Page view activity
- Amount of time on website
- Relative proportion of new visitors to website
- Relative proportion of return visitors to website
- Travel downloads (e.g. download of suggested itineraries)
- Number of contacts built (e.g. those who provide email address to attraction)

The information gathered in these web analytics will aid in bolstering marketing ROI.

ATTRACTING VISITORS

Assignment

Log-in to an analytics site such as *Google Analytics* and explore the metrics surrounding your website. Compare the current statistics to your desired outcome. Create a strategy to close that gap. Consider hiring a consultant specializing in website analytics and who is familiar with ecotourism.

Section V

Caring for Your Site's Ecosystem

Our guests might be visiting our operations for many different reasons, but the ecosystems we manage are probably the biggest draw. Sure, in a large traveling party everyone will have different interests, but they all are drawn to nature.

We understand the need for human-made infrastructure in facilitating visitors' experiences, but sensitivity with regard to the location, design, and size cannot be overstated. Human-made structures should not compete with the resources but simply aid in the visitor's journey. The operation's environmental consciousness should be evident in the services, policies, and product selection employed by the site.

Some visitors might know more than we do on an environmental subject, so we must train our staff to understand the environmental inventory of the site and how it is managed. Examples of areas in which knowledge is needed include exotic plant removal, mowing rotations, visitor carrying capacities, and other land management efforts the operation takes to maintain the ecosystem.

Ecotourists demand authentic experiences in the most genuine places they can find. Fortunately, for us and them, our sites fall into this category. These outdoor classrooms offer a lesson on how the land influenced the people and how the people influenced the land. Popular terms like climate change and carbon footprint can be better understood, so, when our visitors depart our operations, they will not only celebrate Earth Day but may dedicate themselves to an earth life.

Of course, there are many environmental techniques and practices that are particular to each setting or region. Nevertheless, we offer the ones in this section as a way to start a conversation with your team as stewards of the environment.

1	2	3	4	5	6	7	8	9	10
11	12	13	14	15	16	17	18	19	20
21	22	23	24	25	26	27	28	29	30
31	32	33	34	35	36	37	38	39	40
41	42	43	44	45	46	47	48	49	50
51	52	53	54	55	56	57	58	59	60
61	62	63	64	65	66	67	68	69	70
71	72	73	74	75	76	77	78	79	80
81	82	83	84	85	86	87	88	89	90
91	**92**	**93**	**94**	**95**	**96**	**97**	**98**	**99**	**100**
101	**102**	**103**	**104**	**105**	**106**	**107**	**108**	**109**	**110**
111	**112**	113	114	115	116	117	118	119	120
121	122	123	124	125	126	127	128	129	130
131	132	133	134	135	136	137	138	139	140
141	142	143	144	145	146	147	148	149	150
151	152	153	154	155	156	157	158	159	160
161	162	163	164	165	166	167	168	169	170
171	172	173	174	175	176	177	178	179	180

Technique #91

Foster Harmony with the Environment

The overall atmosphere / appearance of any on-site building (gift shop, restaurant, registration area) should be in harmony with your natural setting. This is a critical part of complementing the environmental landscape and not competing with it. Compare harsh lighting from fixtures to natural lighting through windows and doors. Compare a trendy color palette to natural hues.

CARING FOR THE ECOSYSTEM

Assignment

Keenly observe each space with your senses (touch, sound, smell, and sight) to determine if the vibe is in harmony with the natural or cultural resources you are offering. If this process does not come naturally to you, enlist a colleague to assist.

Technique #92

Identify and Map Ecosystems

Plant communities are areas within your operation that plants grow together for a reason. Soil, terrain, amount of sunlight, and moisture are just a few parameters that create these ecosystems. Plant communities within your operation can be smaller than an acre to hundreds or thousands of acres in size. Many ecotourism sites have a diverse and interesting array of flora and may also contain various ecosystems and ecotones which are transition zones between ecosystems.[26]

CARING FOR THE ECOSYSTEM

Assignment

Carefully identify and map all plant communities within your operation. If this is not a skill set within your staff, there are plenty of other sources for assistance. Hire an environmental consulting firm, partner with a college or university, or seek out garden clubs and environmental habitat groups for assistance. Such efforts can be undertaken through the organization of a bioblitz.[1]

Technique #93

Organize a Coordinated Invasive Plant Removal Effort

If a particular non-native invasive plant species is beginning to choke-out native plant species, mobilize a team for manual (herbicide-free) removal. Such a team could comprise a group of volunteers such as a scouting group or the attraction's Friends Group (Citizen Support Organization). Alternatively, all visitors hiking on a particular weekend could be offered bags and instructions regarding how to identify, pick, and dispose of the invasive species.

CARING FOR THE ECOSYSTEM

Assignment

Discuss with the team whether your attraction has an invasive plant species. If so, develop a strategy for chemical-free removal by harnessing the power of a collective effort. This process can be a fun and coordinated initiative by enlisting the aid of volunteers to help.

Technique #94

Actively Manage Carrying Capacity

In many natural settings, there are times in which large visitor volumes strain the sites' ecosystems, and other times during which there are very few visitors. As such, the team should derive creative tactics for enticing some visitors who typically visit during peak periods to instead visit during off-peak periods.

CARING FOR THE ECOSYSTEM

Assignment

Assemble the team and ask these questions: When are the busiest periods? When are the slowest periods? What creative marketing or pricing strategies can be used to shift some of the peak time visitors to slower periods? If this does not produce the desired results, consider reducing visitors in certain areas at environmentally-based selected times of the year. Current and future generations of visitors will appreciate your efforts.

Technique #95

Rotate Mowing Schedules and Mow Less

A carefully groomed lawn can look visually pleasing to some but consider that grassy areas left natural can serve as needed habitat for butterflies and bees. These benefits should be communicated to visitors so that they do not perceive reduced mowing as a lack of care by a site's staff. Rotate these areas yearly for optimum biological benefit.

CARING FOR THE ECOSYSTEM

Assignment

Look for grassy areas within your operation that are not near a facility that might be appropriate options. Gather the team to discuss whether these areas that are currently being mowed or bush-hogged should be left natural for a growing season.

Technique #96

Seed with Optimal Blend

Ground cover seeding is typically needed when soil is disturbed due to occurrences such as building construction, pipe trenching, or utility easement work. When seeding is needed, there are many products on the market. Some grasses, wildflowers, or other ground cover will complement the health of your existing flora and fauna better than others. Some seed blends can even increase the likelihood of positive wildlife viewing as they graze on the ground cover.

CARING FOR THE ECOSYSTEM

Assignment

Are there any areas of your site that need to be seeded or re-seeded? If so, is someone on staff knowledgeable about seed blends? If not, is there an expert such as a university agricultural extension agent that can be contacted? Often the best blends are the ones that are produced locally. This local selection assures that the specific plants grow in your area and that local wildlife use it for food or habitat.

Technique #97

Educate Regarding the Effects of Climate Change

If the ecotourism site is experiencing any detrimental effects due to climate change, such effects should be included in interpretive programming. It can prove educational for visitors to view firsthand the impacts of climate change. Discussing your area's past climate change events and the associated effects should be considered.

CARING FOR THE ECOSYSTEM

Assignment

Team to discuss whether the site has tangible effects due to climate change. If so, how can these effects be incorporated into the educational narratives? This subject can be politically divisive, so presenting only scientifically proven facts will be the best course of action.

Technique #98

Plan Environmental Restoration Projects

The closer your operation is to an urban center, the greater the chances are that more negative human disturbance can be found on the land. These disturbances can be so significant that the original plant community is either no longer present or severely out of its biological norms and is not providing the greatest bio-diversity possible. Full or partial restoration of a plant community to its original state can take generations and be very costly. However, with some plant communities, a little effort and investment now may provide some environmental benefit in years and even more in the decades to come.

> CARING FOR THE ECOSYSTEM

Assignment

When mapping plant communities of your site, there may be areas that cannot be identified as a particular plant community. Map these areas and plan to investigate them further. You may decide three things to do with these areas: 1) keep as is with no additional plans, 2) keep as is for a future development area, or 3) fully or partially restore the area. Consider meeting with an environmental consultant, college, university, or a local authority on your restoration project.

Technique #99

Foster a Living Classroom Philosophy

The ecotourism site should be conceptualized as a "living classroom." That is, any educational cohort ranging from university-level graduate students to preschool students can be invited to study the flora, fauna, and other natural features so long as they do so through non-invasive observation-based methods. Such a living classroom philosophy has many positive outcomes such as an increased interest in and care for the site and its ecosystem.

CARING FOR THE ECOSYSTEM

Assignment

Team to discuss what educational entities currently utilize the site. Should such activities be expanded? For instance, wildlife blinds can be fabricated using recycled building materials and will serve not only as a non-invasive observation-based method but will illustrate your site's commitment to the environment.

Technique #100

Provide Eco-friendly Interior Lighting Options

Interior lighting is an effective way to provide visitor safety, productive workspace, and to create the desired atmosphere for your staff and visitors. Modern eco-friendly lighting options such as LED can reduce energy use, provide more light, create less heat, and can reduce operating costs. Existing fixtures might be retrofitted but if replacement is needed, select fixtures that complement your theme.

> CARING FOR THE ECOSYSTEM

Assignment

During normal operation times of each facility, note the effectiveness of the current lighting fixtures and bulb types. Motion and light sensors can reduce energy use and communicate the right message to visitors. A lighting contractor might be helpful in suggesting the best lighting solutions for your operation.

Technique #101

Have at Least One Solar Panel or Photocell

Due to initial expenses, it might not be feasible to convert to a renewable energy source, such as solar, on a large scale at your operation. Nevertheless, there are a number of solar options that can be adopted on a smaller scale; for instance, converting to solar on only one of your buildings, or outdoor lighting or signage that is powered by photocells connected directly to the product. Having such items at your attraction not only saves money in the long run but also serves to communicate to visitors your care for the environment (and encourages them to do the same).

> CARING FOR THE ECOSYSTEM

Assignment

Discuss with your team if your operation currently uses any renewable energy such as solar. If not, how can renewables be incorporated? For example, can exterior lighting powered by photocells be installed? There are many new technologies powered by solar that could be potentially useful to an ecotourism attraction. Moreover, photocell technology has not only dropped in price but has increased in reliability. If you and your team are not familiar with available products, perhaps you can talk to operators at other sites who have already adopted some solar-powered products.

Technique #102

Consider the Environment in Merchandise and Vendor Selections

If the ecotourism site sells merchandise, ecofriendly products and vendors should be procured whenever possible. Examples might include vendors that are local and have great environmental ethics. Your visitors will likely appreciate your selection of vendors that use reclaimed, recycled, and/or locally sourced materials.

CARING FOR THE ECOSYSTEM

Assignment

Team to discuss current souvenir product lines. Research each vendor to understand their environmental ethics. Ask them to explain their sourcing chain and other important questions. Do the offerings align with the environmental consciousness of the ecotourism attraction?

Technique #103

Create a Take / Leave Station

Often, your visitors will bring an item that they will use during their visit to your operation. These items can be a "one-time use" for visitors and the chance that they will be used "back home" is very low. Sunhats, walking-sticks, diving masks, snow apparel, and many other items and gear seem normal at your operation but are unique to the visitor.

> CARING FOR THE ECOSYSTEM

Assignment

To help the environment, your visitors, and improve reduce/reuse/recycle credibility, set up a take / leave station. This should be a self-serve closet or bin located in the visitor center, check-in, or other convenient location within the operation. Inside a building and near a staff member's work area is preferable.

Technique #104

Donate Environmental Education Packages

Like most businesses or organizations within a local community, ecotourism attractions receive solicitations for donations by other local groups on a routine basis. For instance, high school extracurricular clubs periodically go out and seek donations to be included in their fundraiser auctions. Saying 'no' to such requests does not strengthen community relationships. As such, a win-win would be to donate various environmental education packages. The packages could include on-site and/or off-site interpretive programming. It is recommended that the full price value of the package be printed on it, so that the recipient understands that s/he is receiving a donation of significant value.

CARING FOR THE ECOSYSTEM

Assignment

Does your site already offer environmental education packages? If so, would these current packages be suitable to serve as donation collateral? If not, how can environmental education packages be structured? Should the ones that are used as donations have a restriction in which they cannot be redeemed during peak times?

The team should discuss how donation requests are handled: is everyone on the same page regarding how to respond? Are responses timely and consistent?

Technique #105

Proactively Care for Live Animal Exhibits

Live animal exhibits are a popular way to educate visitors about fauna and ecosystems. Fish, reptiles, birds, and mammals are most common. Special attention needs to be given to these exhibits. Always have a plan and provisions to move an animal quickly off exhibit. Sick, injured, or animals that do not get along well may be a distraction for your visitors.

> CARING FOR THE ECOSYSTEM

Assignment

List the pros and cons of such a live animal exhibit including permits, cost, perceived value to visitors, political issues, and general welfare. Based upon this analysis, decide to keep, expand, minimize, eliminate, or add exhibits. Create areas not in the line of vision of visitors (off exhibit) where such animals can be cared for privately.

Technique #106

Look Out for Rare or Threatened Flora and Fauna

Your operation may have more rare, threatened, or endangered flora and fauna than you may be aware of. Many plants and animals are residents of your area, but some can be seasonal while others only exist after significant natural events such as a fire, severe temperature change, flooding, or other forces. If you and your staff can identify such flora and fauna, they can be better protected.

CARING FOR THE ECOSYSTEM

Assignment

Train staff members to identify rare flora and fauna within your operation. Provide staff with the preferred habitat, time of year, and time of day where they might be seen. Create a flora and fauna sighting whiteboard. This interactive "find and seek" board is fun and educational for staff and visitors. There could be several of these whiteboards anywhere visitors or staff gather.

Technique #107

Study Your Site's Environmental History

Environmental history in this context refers to the relationship humans had on the land and the land had on humans. Knowing your operation's environmental history can help you identify rare plant communities or a unique and historic human use of the land. Such knowledge will not only help you and your team effectively manage the ecosystem but is also useful in infusing interesting content into your educational and interpretive programming.

CARING FOR THE ECOSYSTEM

Assignment

Carefully identify and map environmental history within your operation. If this is not a skill set within your staff, there are plenty of other sources for assistance. For example, potential options might include hiring an environmental consulting firm, partnering with a college or university, or seeking out historical societies and environmental habitat groups for assistance. Because defining the boundaries of each environmental history site is difficult, more than one professional, historical, and environmental opinion may be consulted.

Technique #108

Know the Most Likely Historical Hotspots

You may have heard that real estate is all about three things: location, location, and location. Within your operation, cultures may have inhabited the same location for sometimes hundreds or thousands of years. It is not uncommon on a bluff along a river to find a modern picnic area. Inches under the ground there, one could find a U.S. Civilian Conservation Corps 1933-1942 camping area; inches under that, a settlement from the 1700s; and inches under that, a village of the original inhabitants. The environmental commonality is the river bluff.

> CARING FOR THE ECOSYSTEM

Assignment

Identify areas on a map, like the river bluff described above, that are known or have the greatest likelihood within your operation, to have environmental history. Place this map in a prominent location so staff can easily access it. The map itself will be a reminder of the potential that may lie literally just under their feet.

Technique #109

Protect Potential Artifacts

Training staff members on environmental history within your operation is quintessentially important. This knowledge will not only help them communicate this history but protect it as well. For example, the location of this environmental history can sometimes be in close proximity to maintenance staff and construction contractors as they repair or install underground utilities.

> CARING FOR THE ECOSYSTEM

Assignment

Create a protocol for all staff members and construction contractors that involves any digging. The protocol could include the requirement of a designated staff member to be present when digging is occurring. The staff member should be familiar with what to look for in both environmental evidence as well as human evidence. If something of interest is found or unexplained, experts could be brought in for further investigation.

Technique #110

Plan a Signature Celebration on Earth Day

For more than 50 years, Earth Day has been – and continues to be - the globally recognized day that honors and celebrates environmental protection. All providers of ecotourism offerings are celebrated on the day. Therefore, your ecotourism site should plan a creative and unique "signature celebration" that can become an annual tradition for your team and your visitors.

CARING FOR THE ECOSYSTEM

Assignment

Team to discuss what is currently being done to celebrate Earth Day at your site. Are current Earth Day offerings sufficient or are more creative and unique ideas warranted? Make this event impactful for your visitors and not just another event.

Technique #111

Install a Water Fountain with a Bottle Filler

While theoretically, all water fountains can refill a water bottle, some models have specifically designed bottle fillers. One advantage to this type of water fountain is that it is easier to fill a bottle with this design than with a traditionally-designed fountain. The major advantage, however, is that this design typically has a meter that displays to the user the number of plastic bottles that have been saved from use by people utilizing this particular refilling station.

While there are likely some situations in which we all use disposable plastic bottles, we should raise awareness surrounding the importance of minimizing those situations. A one-time-use plastic bottle takes a minimum of 450 years to biodegrade. Thus, the fountain with the bottle filler helps contribute to this awareness.[27]

CARING FOR THE ECOSYSTEM

Assignment

How old are your site's current water drinking fountains? Could it make financial sense to replace them now? If not, when should they be replaced? There are a variety of water fountains with water bottle fill components on the market – many of which have a meter displaying the number of plastic bottles saved.

Technique #112

Actively Communicate the Site's Environmental Consciousness

Celebrate your operation's sustainability-related success with your visitors and community through your website, video, or written communications. Topics can include how the operation reduces waste, reuses building materials, and recycles. In addition, topics such as alternative power supplies, electric car charging stations, and your reduction of your carbon footprint will be very interesting to your visitors and may inspire further progress.

CARING FOR THE ECOSYSTEM

Assignment

Team to discuss what environmental-related information can be bolstered on the website and how such information can also be disseminated through other communication channels as well. Synthesize this information into a well-crafted success story for your site.

Section VI

Keeping Visitors Safe

When we think of visitor safety, we often think of preventing slips and falls and other routine occurrences that we could find at most establishments. Some operations in natural settings, however, could have many more potential dangers to avoid. Extreme temperatures alone account for thousands of emergencies each year. If our visitors have never spent a winter morning at 1° F or a summer afternoon at 99° F, they may not know what precautions to take. Also, in extreme environments, mountain climbing, scuba diving, hiking, swimming, and other activities can each present unique sets of risks.

The traveling public is not always aware of our local conditions that may cause them health issues. They are sometimes preoccupied with enjoying themselves on their adventure and personal safety may not be on top-of-minds. The best customer service we could possibly deliver is to help keep our visitors safe: safe from operational and environmental hazards and sometimes even from themselves.

Planning, training, and practicing for everything from small emergencies to natural disasters is paramount for visitor safety. Severe storms, a lost child, food allergies, and many more possible examples can arise in our operations. Consequently, our teams should be prepared.

In addition, security of our visitors' belongings, personal information, and financial information is expected to be protected. When our visitors feel safe and secure, they are more likely to relax and fully immerse themselves in the natural and cultural resources we are providing.

Finally, communicating our operations' emergency plans to our visitors, staff, and local response agencies will provide a level of comfort that reinforces the professionalism of our operations.

1	2	3	4	5	6	7	8	9	10
11	12	13	14	15	16	17	18	19	20
21	22	23	24	25	26	27	28	29	30
31	32	33	34	35	36	37	38	39	40
41	42	43	44	45	46	47	48	49	50
51	52	53	54	55	56	57	58	59	60
61	62	63	64	65	66	67	68	69	70
71	72	73	74	75	76	77	78	79	80
81	82	83	84	85	86	87	88	89	90
91	92	93	94	95	96	97	98	99	100
101	102	103	104	105	106	107	108	109	110
111	112	**113**	**114**	**115**	**116**	**117**	**118**	**119**	**120**
121	**122**	**123**	**124**	**125**	**126**	**127**	**128**	**129**	**130**
131	**132**	**133**	**134**	**135**	136	137	138	139	140
141	142	143	144	145	146	147	148	149	150
151	152	153	154	155	156	157	158	159	160
161	162	163	164	165	166	167	168	169	170
171	172	173	174	175	176	177	178	179	180

Technique #113

Ensure the Proper Placement of Roadway Signs

The safety of visitors on your roads and parking areas is a top priority. Sign type and location is something to mindfully consider. Signs placed to be seen while the driver is encountering a turn, hill, dip, or obstacle could be distracting and dangerous to the driver. Negotiating the obstacle should be the driver's priority.

VISITOR SAFETY

Assignment

Take inventory of your roadway and parking lot signs. Note if any sign is currently placed within the caution area described above. If so, consider relocating signs to a relatively flat, straight area before or after the obstacle.

Technique #114

Enhance Safety with Roadway Markings

Painted markings on your roadways and parking areas are most likely regulated by a government entity. These markings such as painted strips between parking spaces and dashed lines between a divided road are expected by today's visitors and aid in fostering a sense of order. Additional markings may benefit your visitors and your operation. For instance: 1) campsite numbers marked on asphalt may replace a site marker often damaged by campers; 2) a solid white line on the edge of the roadway helps define the extent of the roadway for visitor safety; 3) a painted crosswalk helps drivers prepare for pedestrians.

VISITOR SAFETY

Assignment

Review your operation's roadways and parking areas. Identify locations that may benefit from painted roadway markings. Look for signs that can be replaced or enhanced by appropriate markings. Note the locations to be painted and use special roadway paint.

Technique #115

Patrol Campgrounds

The dynamics in a campground can change every night; similar to how dynamics can change as people enter and exit a room. In this regard, a campground is more like a room with people than a hotel with rooms. To minimize potential issues, park staff must be seen patrolling the area. Addressing issues early is wise management.

VISITOR SAFETY

Assignment

On busy days, or on days that typically produce "issues," walk the campground. By not using your vehicle and walking, you can use a combination of senses (visual, audio, and smell) to sometimes detect possible issues before they escalate. Take this time to interact with campers and be seen.

Technique #116

Actively Look for Tree Hazards

Your staff works hard maintaining the grounds that your visitors enjoy. Trails, roads, parking lots, campsites, and other outdoor gathering areas are often very tidy, but we must also routinely look up. Dead or dying trees and limbs can fall unexpectedly and damage facilities and can also injure or kill visitors and staff members.

VISITOR SAFETY

Assignment

Remind staff to look up. This sounds easy, but it is an area that is often overlooked. On a regular basis, have a different person each time study the canopy of the trees above these areas to look for dying, injured, or dead limbs. If a limb is identified for removal, close off the area until it is safe.

Technique #117

Provide Adequate Exterior Lighting Where Needed

Exterior lighting is mostly used at night to identify or luminate selected areas of your operation. Buildings, entrances, pathways, parking lots and signs are often illuminated to benefit the visitor experience. Modern lighting options such as LED can provide more light, create less heat, and can reduce operating costs. It is important to note, however, that special consideration should be given to operations where a "dark sky" is an important part of the visitors' experience.

VISITOR SAFETY

Assignment

During nighttime operations, review the effectiveness of the current lighting in the areas used by visitors at night. Study the fixture, bulb type, and mounting height. Is it too bright, not bright enough, or just right? A lighting contractor might be helpful in suggesting the best lighting solutions for your operation.

Technique #118

Plan for Emergency Response

Emergencies of varying magnitudes transpire within our operation on a routine basis. The same emergency in an urban setting can be less complicated to respond to than in the wilderness. Many variables such as terrain, logistics, and personnel dictate that a written plan should be devised for all possibilities.

VISITOR SAFETY

Assignment

Identify all personnel and outside agencies that may assist if an emergency occurs and invite them to participate. Together, write an emergency operation plan that may include all possible emergencies and all assets (personnel/equipment) available for a response. Make this plan available to all staff members.

Technique #119

Create a Rescue Helicopter Landing Zone

The distance your operation is from a hospital or the ruggedness of the terrain may deem ground transportation of injured visitors impractical. A rescue helicopter landing zone (LZ) can be identified and the location provided to staff, rescue personnel and the helicopter pilots. Depending on the size of your operation, additional LZs may be recommended.

VISITOR SAFETY

Assignment

Working with your local air traffic authorities, select one or more locations within your operation as a helicopter landing zone. An LZ may be near an internal trail or road so the injured visitor may be more easily transported to the LZ. Often, an LZ is located within the proximity of a visitor use area but far enough that a helicopter may function with minimal interference to other visitors.

Technique #120

Use an Incident Response System

Responding or assisting others in an emergency requires planning, training, and practice. Every staff member should have basic training to assist in the event of an emergency. A widely accepted system designed to manage an emergency is the Incident Command System (ICS). This system has many levels and disciplines that can be tailored to your operation.

VISITOR SAFETY

Assignment

Using ICS or an equivalent system, require staff to complete training at a designated level equal to their level of involvement during an emergency. An example of such a system can be found at training.fema.gov. Consider taking ICS100 online to familiarize yourself and staff with the ICS.

Technique #121

Minimize Tripping Hazards

Unimproved trails, such as nature trails or hiking trails, are an important amenity to your operation. As popularity increases on a given trail, the topsoil will likely erode exposing tree roots, boulders, and other sub-soil objects. These roots and boulders can create an obstacle or hazard for visitors. Addressing such obstacles by staff is situational because sometimes these exposed hazards act to maintain soil levels and prevent further erosion.

VISITOR SAFETY

Assignment

Walk each trail routinely and choose to maintain or remove these hazards and monitor the affected areas for erosion and repair as needed. Determine if the risk of keeping the roots and boulders in place for trail integrity is greater than the benefit of reducing or removing them for visitor safety.

Technique #122

Keep Camper Information Secure

A campsite does not offer an occupant the same level of privacy as a hotel. This reality is expected by most of the camping community. However, the information regarding campsite occupants should be held in the strictest confidentiality by staff. Not only credit card numbers but every aspect of the camper's identity and personal information should be handled responsibly.

VISITOR SAFETY

Assignment

Establish and maintain a policy of strict confidentiality regarding campers' names and information. This is more than just a camper courtesy; it helps ensure camper safety. You can never be sure of someone's intent if they inquire about a family on a campsite. Help keep your campers safe.

Technique #123

Provide Regulatory Signs Per Code

Roadways and parking areas are an important part of your operation. They provide access to many of your programs and facilities. Roadway and parking lot regulatory signs are most likely governed by a uniform traffic code. Typically, these codes are administered by the department of transportation or another similar agency. These codes will govern all aspects of the regulatory signs including height, size, font, letter color, background color, reflectivity, and other variables.

VISITOR SAFETY

Assignment

Research the uniform traffic sign regulations and the agency that governs your operation. Carefully review your roadway and parking lot regulatory signs to help ensure that they meet the required codes. Invite the governing agency out to visit your operation for a courtesy review of your roadway signs.

Technique #124

Minimize the Likelihood of Foodborne Illness

Everyone who serves food at your site whether it be members of your team, a 3rd party contractor (vendor), or a caterer contracted for a specific event, must take food safety seriously. They each must be trained and properly certified in food handling in accord with local regulations and ordinances. Go to FDA.com and/or your local health department for more information.[28]

VISITOR SAFETY

Assignment

What systems are in place to ensure that anyone serving food at your attraction is trained and certified in accord with current regulations and ordinances? Are those systems adequate? Keep food handling training records on all employees and require all food providers to do the same.

Technique #125

Plan for a Lost Visitor

A lost child or lost grandparent is a bad situation that can often get worse without a quick response. The longer it takes to find the individuals, the further they can potentially stray into the wilderness. This common issue requires a written plan, training, and practice by all staff members. This first type of search is typically known as a "hasty search". Each staff member will have a different role, but they will all be part of the successful outcome.

> VISITOR SAFETY

Assignment

Create and practice procedures that can be immediately put into action by all staff members. The procedure should include a staff member staying with the family of the lost person and keeping them informed on the progress of the search. Go to FEMA.gov for more information surrounding these procedures.

Technique #126

> **Know How to Coordinate with Professional Search and Rescue**

Search and Rescue (SAR) is an established discipline of trained professionals and volunteers dedicated to this field. Types of SAR include ground, mountain, cave, snow, urban, wilderness, water, and others. If the "hasty search" does not reveal the lost visitor(s), a trained SAR team will be needed. Go to FEMA.gov for more information.[29]

VISITOR SAFETY

Assignment

Understand the difference between a "hasty search" for a lost individual and a professional search and rescue situation. Identify your local search and rescue provider and offer your operation as a venue for them to train. Ask how your team can participate.

Technique #127

Provide Loaner Recreational Safety Equipment

The safety of your visitors is paramount. Sometimes visitors will forget to bring their recreational safety equipment. Other times, they may not realize that this equipment is required in their visit to your operation. Making loaner recreational safety equipment available helps keep your visitors safe.

VISITOR SAFETY

Assignment

Make loaner safety equipment available to all visitors. Items such as bicycle helmets and personal floatation devices (PFDs) will be greatly appreciated by visitors. Ask staff members and recreational service providers what are the common safety items most forgotten by visitors?

Technique #128

Prepare Your Visitors for a Natural Disaster

There are many types of natural disasters in the world: typhoons, tsunamis, mud slides, earthquakes, river flooding, drought, tornado, red tide, volcano eruptions, hurricanes, wildfires, snow slides and more. Your visitors are not only from down the road but across the globe. Many visitors, while on vacation, do not actively track the weather or follow the latest news while traveling.

> VISITOR SAFETY

Assignment

Assume that your visitors do not know how to prepare for and survive a natural disaster that may be relatively common in the area of your operation (in comparison to where the visitors live). When appropriate, in a non-alarming manner, communicate with your visitors well before they will have to act. Subsequently, assist them as needed.

Technique #129

Have an Automated External Defibrillator (AED) Readily Available

In the U.S., all 50 states have enacted laws or regulations pertaining to which establishments AEDs are required. Most states, however, only mandate them to be in schools or in places such as health clubs were people exercise. Even if the state in which your attraction is located does not require you to have an AED, it is good practice to invest in one (or more than one) and have it readily available. The cost of AEDs has dropped significantly in recent years and are affordable for most operators.

VISITOR SAFETY

Assignment

Does your site currently have at least one AED? If so, does everyone on your team know where it is located? Are there staff members certified to use it (First aid discussed later in this section)?

If you do not currently have an AED, could you invest in the purchase of one (or more than one for expansive operations)? Because there are numerous types on the market, consult with your local rescue squad about the best model/brand to purchase. Once purchased, also consult with your local rescue squad about where it should be located and what signage should be installed to denote its location. Often, AEDs are stored in alarmed cases so that they are not tampered with or stolen.

Technique #130

Remain Knowledgeable about Options for Medical or Dietary Needs

Some of our visitors will have special medical and dietary needs that we must pay close attention to. Visitors' daily routines managing these issues are sometimes thrown in-flux when they are away from home. All staff members should be able to direct these visitors, so they can meet their medical and dietary needs.

VISITOR SAFETY

Assignment

Consider providing commonly requested items for medical and dietary needs or have the knowledge to direct visitors regarding where to locate these items or services. Work with your team to create a list of items to keep on hand, or, at a minimum, provide them with the locations in your community.

Technique #131

Get Involved with After Hours Emergencies

When there is a law enforcement or medical emergency in the campground, lodge, or other overnight accommodation area, the staff of the operation may not be involved in the response. If the visitor calls the emergency number directly after normal operation hours, staff may not know of the issue until they arrive in the morning.

VISITOR SAFETY

Assignment

Periodically meet with the responding law enforcement and medical providers and ask to be notified when responding to your operation. Invite them to your operation for a tour or offer your site as a training location to further the relationship.

Technique #132

Design an On-Call Telephone System

Although hotels and motels, ecolodges, campgrounds, and other overnight accommodations are 24-hour operations, your site may not be staffed overnight. In some circumstances, this staff interruption can cause your visitors to feel vulnerable and maybe even unappreciated. This can result in a missed opportunity to provide great customer service.

VISITOR SAFETY

Assignment

Provide an "on-call" cell phone to a designated staff member that will be on-call through hours of unstaffed operation. This added responsibility should rotate through a few staff members who live on-site or close by and are familiar with all aspects of your operation. While each on-call staff member may have their own cell phone, using one on-call cell phone will only require visitors to be provided with one phone number.

Technique #133

Reduce the Likelihood of Dangerous Wildlife Encounters

While a certain number of alarming wildlife encounters are almost unavoidable, some can be circumvented. For example, bear proof garbage receptacles will reduce the frequency of close encounters between humans and bears. In many jurisdictions, animals that are habituated with the offerings of our trash are often relocated from the area at best.

VISITOR SAFETY

Assignment

Discuss with your team whether adequate measures are currently in place to minimize dangerous wildlife encounters. Are all installed safety mechanisms currently operable? Do additional devices need to be installed? Should visitors be given additional instruction upon their arrival such as not to feed the wildlife?

Technique #134

Know First Aid

Due to factors such as rugged terrain, adventurous activities and sometimes harsh environmental conditions, our staff and visitors can be injured while at our operations. Sustaining injuries should be considered more a matter of "when it will happen" as opposed to "if it will happen". Knowing first aid, therefore, is an important component of our profession.

VISITOR SAFETY

Assignment

Set a minimum requirement for staff members to be certified in a first aid/CPR/AED course of your choice. You could also select a smaller group of staff to be certified at a higher level such as advanced first aid, water rescue, and/or wilderness first aid. The American Red Cross, as well as other organizations, may deliver regularly scheduled classes in your area. If not, offer to host a course at your operation.

Technique #135

Reduce Occurrences of Slip and Fall Incidents

Flooring that is particularly slippery when wet can often be made less so. Unpainted wooden decking boards, for instance, can be more routinely power washed to remove the build-up of a slippery film. Painted flooring surfaces, whether wood, concrete, or cement, can be given an additional coat of paint with some sand or finely-ground walnut shells mixed into the paint. Anti- slip tape and rugs are additional alternatives.

VISITOR SAFETY

Assignment

Discuss with your coworkers: Are any of the site's flooring surfaces particularly slippery when wet? If so, what measures can be taken to alleviate this safety hazard? Do not forget to look up and see if a tree is shading the surface, providing an ideal habitat for algae and mold.

Section VII

Maximizing the Operational Efficiencies of Your Site

Maximizing the operational efficiencies of our sites can benefit our operations in numerous ways. Doing so could save time and money while making the experience for the visitor easier and more enjoyable. The two greatest sources for identifying problem areas and potential solutions are our visitors and staff. For some operations, inviting an expert for a particular issue would be advisable.

In some cases, the physical flow of a site can be enhanced to increase visitor satisfaction. Guests do not like to wait in line, and, if they do have to wait, they want to be comfortable. If there is a delay or equipment issue, visitors can feel reassured by direct communications from a staff member.

Confusing signs, directions, and information can cause frustration for our guests and staff members. Moreover, a modern, efficient point-of-sales system with a safe credit card interface is a must in today's market. The "ease of transaction" signals a professional operation and provides a level of comfort for the customer.

Also, to facilitate operational efficiencies, day-to-day decision making as well as long term planning can be done collaboratively with all involved parties. Master plans, operation plans, and business plans facilitated by a consultant are helpful to achieve team buy-in. Professional research and surveys can provide a wealth of knowledge and can create a foundation for effective decision making and inputs into these plans.

Visitor service providers such as food concessions, horse liveries, and equipment rentals can really enhance the visitors' experiences within our operations. They must, however, contribute to and not detract from our operational efficiencies. Mutually agreed upon values and goals will go a long way in fostering life-long positive memories for our visitors.

1	2	3	4	5	6	7	8	9	10
11	12	13	14	15	16	17	18	19	20
21	22	23	24	25	26	27	28	29	30
31	32	33	34	35	36	37	38	39	40
41	42	43	44	45	46	47	48	49	50
51	52	53	54	55	56	57	58	59	60
61	62	63	64	65	66	67	68	69	70
71	72	73	74	75	76	77	78	79	80
81	82	83	84	85	86	87	88	89	90
91	92	93	94	95	96	97	98	99	100
101	102	103	104	105	106	107	108	109	110
111	112	113	114	115	116	117	118	119	120
121	122	123	124	125	126	127	128	129	130
131	132	133	134	135	**136**	**137**	**138**	**139**	**140**
141	**142**	**143**	**144**	**145**	**146**	**147**	**148**	**149**	**150**
151	**152**	**153**	**154**	**155**	**156**	**157**	**158**	159	160
161	162	163	164	165	166	167	168	169	170
171	172	173	174	175	176	177	178	179	180

Technique #136

Identify Congestion Points

At times, your attraction might seem as if it is at maximum carrying capacity, not because it is, but rather because there are 1, 2, or 3 "bottleneck" points. The cause of these bottleneck points can be both physical and operational but with the same negative outcome. In some cases, these congestion points can be alleviated through simple solutions such as additional supplies, cross training of staff, different visitor flows, etc.

OPERATIONAL EFFICIENCY

Assignment

Discuss with your team whether your operation has any congestion points? If so, determine the cause or causes and describe the future condition that would be acceptable. Are there reasonable solutions that can be applied to alleviate such congestion?

Technique #137

Install Efficient Credit Card Technologies

All of the attraction's access points should have technology in place to accept credit card payment. Moreover, whenever possible, credit card technologies should be upgraded to include the fastest and most efficient process feasible. Currently, there is a wide range of credit card technologies on the market with regard to processing speed and ease of use. Even in rural and remote locations, the technology is improving.

OPERATIONAL EFFICIENCY

Assignment

Team to audit current credit card capabilities and add/upgrade where needed. Consult with your bank, data service provider, and your point-of-sales system provider. There is often not a single magic remedy but sometimes a slight upgrade in several components can make a noticeable difference.

Technique #138

Carefully Consider Food Service Options

While serving food can be a useful amenity for visitors and can potentially be profitable, it is important to point out that, many times, it becomes a money-pit for attractions, canceling-out revenues earned in other areas of the site. If an operator feels strongly that food is needed due to the remote location of the attraction or s/he feels strongly that food service can be profitable, then due diligence is needed. Consider, for instance, 1) hiring a consultant to design the food operation and menu; or 2) outsourcing the food operations to a vendor with a proven track record in similar settings.

OPERATIONAL EFFICIENCY

Assignment

If your operation already offers food service, discuss what actions are needed to make it more efficient: 1. Cost effective; 2. Consistent product quality; and 3. Consistent service quality. If you are considering food service, think about how your operation's theme will run through the design, furnishings, and menu items.

Technique #139

Employ Solid Research when Making Resource Allocation Decisions

While, on the surface, this tip appears to be commonsense, the authors of this book have witnessed a number of attractions make mistakes when it comes to resource allocation decisions. Questions often surface such as: would it be better to invest in stand-up paddle boards versus kayaks? Should we build yurts or add more RV camping sites? Properly designed visitor surveys can inform these decisions, but it is easy to design such a survey incorrectly. Some reliable secondary sources can also be useful when making such decisions such as the state's comprehensive outdoor recreation plan (SCORP) which gauges demand for various recreational activities on a 5-year cycle.[30]

OPERATIONAL EFFICIENCY

Assignment

Discuss with the team what research inputs are used when making resource allocation decisions. How can those research inputs be improved? What other research inputs should be considered? Secure a copy of your state's SCORP, and all other states' SCORPs within a 1-2 hour drive of your operation, and review for trends.

Technique #140

Keep a Log of Visitors' Requests

If a log of visitors' requests is kept, not only can adequate follow-up be afforded to a particular request, but also trends can be identified as to what visitors are desiring. Such trends can inform capital investments and resource allocation. This information can be shared with visitor service providers that operate within your site.

OPERATIONAL EFFICIENCY

Assignment

Discuss with the team whether a log of visitors' requests is currently being kept. If not, then how would the logistics work for putting such a system in place? With all that the operational staff is responsible for, remembering to jot-down this information is sometimes the hardest part. Other ways to acquire this information may have to be investigated such as having each staff member relay a visitor request or suggestion at a staff meeting.

Technique #141

Analyze Why a Visitor Volume Forecast Was Incorrect

Even the most experienced site managers produce visitor volume forecasts that are sometimes incorrect. When the visitor volumes are much higher than anticipated, customer service can suffer due to lack of preparation and staffing. Conversely, when visitor volumes are much lower than forecasted, money can be lost through unnecessarily high staffing levels and waste of perishable supplies such as food. Therefore, the first step in reducing future inaccurate forecasting is to analyze the causes of the inaccuracies.[31]

OPERATIONAL EFFICIENCY

Assignment

Discuss with the team why a particular day was much busier or slower than forecasted. Were these deviations from the forecast reasonably foreseeable? What can be done to circumvent this gap between actual and forecasted visitor volumes in the future?

Technique #142

Proactively Manage Perceived Waiting Times

Even with top-rate business volume forecasting, visitors to ecotourism attractions sometimes must have brief periods of waiting as their experiences unfold. It is important to note, however, that a five minute wait can feel like either a seven minute wait or a three minute wait depending upon how it is managed by the service provider. Therefore, strategies should be in place for reducing perceived waiting times by psychologically occupying visitors during waits. Research indicates that even hanging one or more mirrors in areas where people wait can reduce the perceived waiting length.[32]

OPERATIONAL EFFICIENCY

Assignment

Discuss the following with the team: where at your attraction do visitors typically wait? What tactics are in place at those points to psychologically occupy visitors during those waits? What innovative perceived waiting time-reducing tactics can be added?

Technique #143

Offer Text Messaging as an Option for Visitors

Some industries, such as the airline and hotel sectors, have improved their operational efficiencies by allowing their customers to opt-in to receiving certain communications through text messaging. Such a service is particularly appreciated by those who communicate often through text messaging.

It is important to realize that this technique is not feasible for all operations, particularly those located in remote areas with weak or no cell service. Nevertheless, as technologies advance, it should be understood that this is a service that can eventually be implemented.

OPERATIONAL EFFICIENCY

Assignment

Does your operation currently communicate through text messaging with visitors? If not, is this a practice that can be worked towards? Will this work on-site to inform a visitor that their rental item or tour is available? Can you use it for previous visitors to let them know of deals and events?

Technique #144

Assess the Effectiveness of the Operation's Sign Program

In most operations, there are several types of signs maintained at the site. Regulatory, directional, informative, and interpretive signs constitute the majority. Each sign should have been placed with a purpose that is obvious or should become obvious to the visitor once read.

OPERATIONAL EFFICIENCY

Assignment

Invite a person who has never been to your attraction to accompany you on a visit. Let him/her know that you need help in reviewing your sign program. As you drive or walk past each sign, have him/her read and comment on the effectiveness of the sign to you. Make notes of the comments and, if necessary, mark the location of the signs on a map.

Technique #145

Audit the RV Camping Sites

The popularity of the RV industry continues to grow. Todays' RVs are taller, longer, wider, heavier, and require more electric amperage than in the past. If your current campsites can only accommodate the current models, your operation might get behind with the next generation of RV's. If upgrading to current standards, consider anticipating future specifications to stay relevant with the RV trends.

OPERATIONAL EFFICIENCY

Assignment

When the RV campsite is vacant, audit each site to the most recent RV standards. This audit might include measuring the campsite's height of vegetation, the maximum length of the site, the width of the site, and a soil compaction analysis to estimate the maximum weight the site base can hold. Create a plan to modernize as needed.

Technique #146

Create a Maximum Length of Stay

The modern ecotourist is expecting an authentic experience in all aspects of the visit. Campground visitors are especially demanding this authenticity because they have decided to immerse themselves in the natural and cultural resources by camping. Some campgrounds do not have a maximum stay policy that can lead to someone effectively "living" in the campground. A situation in which someone is residing long-term in a campsite next to someone camping for a night or two can cause user conflicts and detract from site authenticity.

OPERATIONAL EFFICIENCY

Assignment

Consider creating a length of stay policy. This policy can change seasonally to accommodate the occupancy rate. For instance, a two week maximum stay when "in season", four weeks during the "shoulder season" and six weeks during the "off-season".

Technique #147

Stock Extra Electrical Receptacles and Breakers

Electric power hookups are an attractive amenity to RV campers. Because so many RV rigs arrive and depart often at each campsite, the electric receptacles and breakers are prone to wearing out more than in typical residential or commercial use. Even if the receptacles are operational, often they can look unsightly with electric burn marks on them.

OPERATIONAL EFFICIENCY

Assignment

Stock replacement electric receptacles and electric breakers in bulk as a convenience for your camping visitors and staff. Train appropriate staff members how to safely test and replace electric receptacles and breakers in night-time conditions. Choose the receptacle color wisely: dark colors hide burn marks and age better visually; however, bright colors are easier to see at night.

Technique #148

Professionally Manage Camper-to-Camper Interface

Campgrounds are more like a room of people than a hotel of rooms in that other campers can hear and see a lot of what goes on in other campsites. This proximity can lead to rumors and gossip within the campground especially in longer term camping situations. It is important that staff invest the time to listen to these comments but not to take the "bait" to join the campground chat.

OPERATIONAL EFFICIENCY

Assignment

Train and practice with your staff on how to handle a situation when campers share comments about other campers. Remember that all campers are visitors in your operation. Practice listening to each other during a training session and learn not to take the bait but to respond professionally.

Technique #149

Light Up as Needed

You may have areas within your operation that are only programmed for day-time activities or for both daytime and night-time activities. Throughout the lifecycle of your operation, these areas may have changed uses. Sometimes there might be lights within your operation that come on each night and are not needed that the staff may not even know about.

OPERATIONAL EFFICIENCY

Assignment

During night-time conditions, inspect your operation to make sure appropriate lighting is being provided in your night-time programmed areas. Also, note if there are lights (from a previous use) in the day-time programmed areas that can be reduced or removed.

Technique #150

Spread a Listening-Post Mentality

When visitors are in public areas of your operation, the staff should be trained to listen for keywords in their conversations incidental to their regular duties. It is quite common for visitors to be discussing their perceptions of your offerings and these perceptions can serve as useful feedback in the spirit of continuous improvement. Many visitors are reluctant to communicate this feedback directly to the service provider.

OPERATIONAL EFFICIENCY

Assignment

Discuss the following with the team: Does a listening-post mentality currently exist? How can it be improved? Provide guidance on respecting the visitor's privacy while listening for key words about your operation. This can also help with customer service by better anticipating the visitor's needs.

Technique #151

Have Pre-Printed Directions Readily Available

Visitors at your operation might ask staff for directions to the same 3-4 popular destinations (examples: camping supplies, vehicle fuel, and post office) each day. Providing verbal directions can take valuable time away from your staff and some visitors might not fully understand the directions.

OPERATIONAL EFFICIENCY

Assignment

Ask your staff to brainstorm the three most asked for destinations. Print the directions on a map and have them available upon request at check-in, visitor centers, and other inside counter operations. These maps can be small and designed to fit in the pockets of staff members.

Technique #152

Have Rainy Day Options Readily Available

During times of poor weather, overnight visitors who come to your operation for adventure may get restless. Loaner books and board games can bring a little sunshine to your visitors' day. Maybe a family-friendly movie can be shown complete with bean-bag-chairs and popcorn. If the children like it, the parents will love it.

OPERATIONAL EFFICIENCY

Assignment

Acquire appropriate books, board games, and movies that would be appreciated by your visitors. The selections should include appropriateness and degree of enjoyment for various age groups. Periodically review the popularity of the selections as trends change.

Technique #153

Measure Visitor Satisfaction

The adage, "If you don't measure it, you can't manage it" applies here. Your attraction should administer a user-friendly visitor survey on an ongoing basis. Survey results should be included in the key performance indicators (KPIs) that are monitored on an ongoing basis by your operation.

OPERATIONAL EFFICIENCY

Assignment

Does your site currently have a visitor survey? Is the survey asking the most important questions? Is it too long? Is the sampling strategy appropriate? What is the current response rate? How are the findings being disseminated?

If you do not currently have a survey, it is recommended that you seek professional guidance from a consultant specializing in your type of operation. Designing an effective survey takes more practice and expertise than many people realize.

Technique #154

Draft a 5-Year Strategic Plan

There are many potential benefits associated with having a 5-year strategic plan. For instance, a plan guiding the direction of strategy can be motivating for the team. Moreover, when applying for grants, many funding agencies require a written plan to help ensure that the grant funds are directed to the most strategic use.

Most (all) state and national parks have master plans that primarily focus on future land use and capital improvements / construction. The strategic plan discussed here would supplement the master plan. Some park systems refer to the park's strategic plan as a "business plan" in which future costs, revenues, and economic impacts are forecasted.

OPERATIONAL EFFICIENCY

Assignment

Discuss whether your attraction currently has a 5-year strategic plan. If not, should the team develop it internally by using other site's plans as templates? Or should a consultant specializing in your type of operation be sought to aid in the strategic process?

Technique #155

Develop an Agreement Template for Contracted Visitor Service Providers

Tour operators, concessionaires, and contractors can enhance the visitor experience and provide a product or service that you are not able to otherwise offer. Managing these opportunities to align with your operation can be accomplished to enhance your brand awareness and visitor satisfaction. It is prudent to note, however, that any entity providing a product or service within your operation needs to do so under appropriate guidance and supervision.

OPERATIONAL EFFICIENCY

Assignment

With advice from your legal counsel, write a standard agreement template that ensures your brand is enhanced through their product or service. Areas like exceptional customer service, environmentally sustainable products and practices, authentic representation of local culture, history and the environment should be clearly identified and understood by all involved.

Technique #156

Develop Standards of Price and Quality for Contracted Visitor Service Providers

Whether through a contracted visitor service provider or part of your internal operation, quality and price points of products or services must be managed through "standards of quality" and "price schedule" guidelines. These documents serve as benchmarks and can be used to compare one price to another or set expectations of quality.

OPERATIONAL EFFICIENCY

Assignment

Carefully research and write these two distinctly different documents, to be shared with your contractors and staff. This may include considering the following questions: Does the product reflect the authenticity of the natural and cultural resources offered? Is this price affordable to most visitors?

Technique #157

Develop a Vision Statement for Contracted Visitor Service Providers

Within our operations, there is a place, time, and accepted way to provide products and services. A unique vision statement should be written and applied to guide contracted or self-providers. Thought should be given to the purpose of providing products or services; will they be for the visitors' needs such as water, sunscreen, and maps? And / or for the visitors' wants such as t-shirts, post cards, or souvenirs?

OPERATIONAL EFFICIENCY

Assignment

Write a vision statement that describes the purpose or benefit of providing products and services to the visitors. Craft a mission statement on how and where products will be offered. There will always be product and service "creep" (a.k.a. evolution), but a sound vision will keep your operation centered.

Technique #158

Create a Culture of Seamless Experience Delivery with Visitor Service Providers

A visitor to your attraction should have a positive and memorable experience whether s/he transacts with a contracted vendor or with a member of your team. In fact, the visitor should not be able to distinguish between the two. That is, the visitor should not be able to tell the difference between a contractor and an internal staff member – both can be equally important in delivering a memorable experience.

OPERATIONAL EFFICIENCY

Assignment

Because this is truly a team effort, both you and the contracted service providers should brainstorm ways to make the experience seamless. For example, what narratives are visitors receiving? What branding and trade dress cues are visitors seeing and hearing?

Section VIII

Engaging with External Audiences

The importance of managing our operations "outside the gates" cannot be overstated. The obvious external group we often focus on is, of course, potential visitors. In many cases, our site is one stop along their journey and is a part of the region and community that they were drawn to explore. These visitors are seeking authentic and genuine experiences; therefore, external communications must accent these attributes.

Relationships with local residents, the stronger our sites' connections are with the community, the more authenticity our offerings have to the ecotourist. Building and maintaining relationships with specific community entities is an important way of continuing the thread of the operation in the tapestry of the community. Some of these community entities are looking for partners and will not take long to form a relationship. There will be other community stakeholders and organizations that will simply take longer. Our patience will often be rewarded as these entities are sometimes the most beneficial to our sites.

Interestingly, if we consider historic towns, cities, and villages in Europe, the common part of them is the plaza ("town square" or "piazza"). The plaza is typically surrounded by important government, religious and community buildings. The plaza is where the people came together as it anchored the community. Hence, we should strive in a certain sense to make our attractions the plaza of the community. Along these lines, we should offer to host meetings and community events. We should invite the local hospitality industry to come and experience the offerings. We should create opportunities for school groups to feel included. Furthermore, we should reinforce cultural heritage and honor local leaders and elders.

As we invite more of the community to our operations, the need to be a part of their events will become ever more important. We should, therefore, provide off-site speakers and interpretation as requested. Strategic alliances can also be created in various forms with the business community. We must remember to publicize our region's assets as well as our own. In summary, genuine relationships with external audiences will reap many rewards.

1	2	3	4	5	6	7	8	9	10
11	12	13	14	15	16	17	18	19	20
21	22	23	24	25	26	27	28	29	30
31	32	33	34	35	36	37	38	39	40
41	42	43	44	45	46	47	48	49	50
51	52	53	54	55	56	57	58	59	60
61	62	63	64	65	66	67	68	69	70
71	72	73	74	75	76	77	78	79	80
81	82	83	84	85	86	87	88	89	90
91	92	93	94	95	96	97	98	99	100
101	102	103	104	105	106	107	108	109	110
111	112	113	114	115	116	117	118	119	120
121	122	123	124	125	126	127	128	129	130
131	132	133	134	135	136	137	138	139	140
141	142	143	144	145	146	147	148	149	150
151	152	153	154	155	156	157	158	**159**	**160**
161	**162**	**163**	**164**	**165**	**166**	**167**	**168**	**169**	**170**
171	**172**	**173**	**174**	**175**	**176**	**177**	**178**	**179**	**180**

Technique #159

Publicize Economic Impacts

The psychological and health benefits associated with visiting and recreating in outdoor settings are widely known; however, the economic impacts are not as commonly known. Such economic impact metrics might include jobs supported, labor income, tax revenue generation, and contributions to the gross domestic product (GDP).[33]

EXTERNAL AUDIENCES

Assignment

Team to discuss whether economic impacts are currently being tabulated on an annual basis. If not, how can this practice be instituted? Contract with a university or consulting practice to calculate the annual economic impacts the attraction has within the state or region. Such economic metrics can prove useful when competing for grants and/or public funding sources.

Technique #160

Apply for Membership in Local Civic or Business Organizations

Regardless if your operation is privately-owned, publicly-owned, or a not-for-profit, your positive relationship with the business community is essential. From sourcing local products and services, to sharing your operation with the business community, a strong symbiotic relationship is critical. In fact, your operation may be the reason many of the other businesses exist.

EXTERNAL AUDIENCES

Assignment

Consider being a member of your local Chamber of Commerce or other business organization. Select a staff member to be a direct liaison with this group. Look for ways to create partnerships that will benefit the natural and cultural resources of your community and operation. At least once per year, invite the group to your operation.

Technique #161

Periodically Host Civic Group Meetings

If your site has a meeting space large enough, periodically host a civic group meeting on a pro-bono basis. You may originally have to invest in furnishings or technologies to support them, but, in the long run, these investments could create a terrific synergy. The benefits of opportunities like this are difficult to calculate but the advantages can last generations.

EXTERNAL AUDIENCES

Assignment

Discuss with your team whether your site currently hosts community group meetings. If yes, is it done routinely and in a fashion that displays your attraction n the best possible light? If you do not currently host meetings, is this a practice that should be instituted?

Technique #162

Utilize Off-Site Interpretation

Cultural, historical, and/or nature-based interpretive programming is common at ecotourism sites. Providers should, however, also consider how such programing can be delivered remotely through "off-site interpretation" at locations such as schools, libraries, and festivals. Doing so would likely introduce the potential to engage with audiences previously unfamiliar with the ecotourism destination.[34] Such mobile interpretation is also important when your attraction must close due to occurrences such as a natural disaster or pandemic. In a case such as this, mobile interpretation can be delivered through a platform such as Zoom.

EXTERNAL AUDIENCES

Assignment

Team to discuss the potential for mobile interpretation: how can it be designed? Who will deliver it and at what locations? Will it be a box full or a trailer full? What will need to be supplied by the host site? Examples include electricity, water, table, and PA systems.

Technique #163

Extend VIP Treatment to Military Veterans

Most would likely agree that military veterans are deserving of special treatment. Ideas might include "veterans' appreciation" days with discounted pricing, preferred parking spots, or some other gesture of gratitude. This can be a permanent offer or on selected days such as Memorial Day, Independence Day, Veterans Day, and others.

EXTERNAL AUDIENCES

Assignment

Team to discuss whether special perks are already extended to veterans. If so, are the perks adequately communicated? If veterans are not currently being recognized, should one or more initiatives be put in place? Consider all scenarios; for instance, if the veteran gets free admission will her/his family pay full price?

Technique #164

Develop an Educators' Advisory Board

Invite 10-12 educators in your area to be appointed to your ecotourism attraction's Educators' Advisory Board. The appointees would serve on a voluntary basis and should range from preschool educators to university-level professors. Creating this Board will: 1) help keep your attraction at the top-of-mind of area educators; and 2) gather their input regarding how to further relationships with area education-based entities. For instance, advice can be gathered regarding whether live stream feeds from your attraction would be of interest to various educators and their students.

EXTERNAL AUDIENCES

Assignment

Team to discuss the logistics of forming this Board: should by-laws be written? How often should it meet? How will Board nominations and appointments be handled? Perhaps Board members should rotate out of their positions on a prescribed schedule but not all at the same time.

Technique #165

Formally Recognize All Volunteers

Once per year, all the site's volunteers should be formally recognized and thanked with a ceremony and certificate. The ceremony should be well-orchestrated with entertainment such as a slideshow of photos taken throughout the year. Local media can be invited to help shine a light on your volunteers which may help recruit future volunteers.

EXTERNAL AUDIENCES

Assignment

Are the volunteers at your attraction formally recognized and thanked each year? If they are not currently being formally recognized, who will plan the ceremony? If they are currently being recognized, can the ceremony be improved through low/no-cost measures such as a slideshow of photos?

Technique #166

Monitor Websites for Accuracy

Quarterly/seasonally, staff should check websites that describe the attraction for accuracy.[35] This also presents a great opportunity to post photos of the previous year's visitors enjoying your offerings during the season you are in. Highlight sights and sounds of your natural and cultural resources at this time of year with short videos.

EXTERNAL AUDIENCES

Assignment

Assign a person or a team of staff members to be in-charge of the operation's website. With detail, review all the technical data; for example, hours of operation, prices, and special event information. Add photos and videos that represent the site during this season so potential visitors can visualize themselves enjoying your operation.

Technique #167

Make it Easy to Book a Group

If someone in the community desires to bring a group to the attraction (school group, family reunion, etc.) the process of making the arrangements should be as efficient for the client as possible. Systems of group booking efficiency should be in place such as a preprinted list of information fields that the team member who receives the inquiry is trained to complete.

Moreover, in the telephone system "please press # to talk to a team member about booking a group event" should be the first or second option presented rather than the 6th or 7th. Likewise, on the website "click here for information about bringing groups" should be in a highly visible location.

EXTERNAL AUDIENCES

Assignment

Are all members of the team trained in how to efficiently handle group business inquiries? Are all team members disseminating consistent and accurate information? Are all inquiries adequately followed-up on and managed in an efficient manner?

Technique #168

Create Strategic Alliances

Visitors are always looking for a good deal. One way to provide this is through strategic alliances with your local business community. There are entities that have a natural connection with your site. They can be businesses that the operation has connection with, business types that are often requested by visitors, and others that would add value for your visitors.

EXTERNAL AUDIENCES

Assignment

Create a program to partner with local businesses that will offer a discount to your visitors when they show they have recently visited your operation. If not a discount, maybe a free upgrade or special "no wait" line. Programs such as this will further connect your community to your operation and your visitors to the community.

Technique #169

Sponsor a Children's Art Contest

It feels good for children to go to a public attraction and see their artwork displayed. Moreover, this positive feeling is as strong – or stronger – for the parents of those children. For most ecotourism sites, there are themes that can be developed for children's art contests that are not only mission-compliant but also help reinforce the natural, historical, and/or cultural significance of the site.

> EXTERNAL AUDIENCES

Assignment

Discuss with your team who will reach out to the local elementary school(s) to organize the art contest. Be sure that the parameters of the program are clear; for example: 1) Will all the submitted artwork be displayed? 2) Where will it be displayed? 3) Does the artwork need to be weather resistant for outdoor display or does your site have enough indoor space to display the submissions? 4) For what timeframe will the submissions be displayed? 5) What will be done with the artwork after the contest is over?

Technique #170

Host Mission-Compliant Festivals and Events

Special events within your operation involving your local community can be a win-win for your community and your visitors. Environmental, heritage, and musical events are popular ways to involve your community and add value to your visitors' experiences. Consider the latest trends of these events but always be true to your site's mission.

EXTERNAL AUDIENCES

Assignment

Meet with local leaders and create a list of events in the area. This can guide you in creating a new original event that will add value to the visitor experience without competing with the community. Survey your visitors during the time of year you are considering an event to gather their input.

Technique #171

Seek and Embrace Native Inhabitants

Chances are that the land your operation sits on has had human occupants for hundreds or even thousands of years. There are likely elders in your community that remember a time before your operation existed or maybe early memories of your attraction. The insights and knowledge possessed by these native inhabitants can be interesting and valuable to your attraction. Moreover, genuine and active support by these locals can only strengthen your operation.

EXTERNAL AUDIENCES

Assignment

Reach out to your community and invite everyone who has a story to tell about the area around your operation or about the operation itself. Invite your community to bring blankets or their favorite chair to sit and listen to the stories. A moderator from your staff will add to the event by asking questions and facilitating from one speaker to another. Add a picnic lunch and a small sound system and you have another annual event including the community. With the appropriate permission, the stories can be recorded for archive purposes.

Technique #172

Offer Familiarization (FAM) Tours to Community Members

Harnessing the ongoing support of your community can provide many benefits to your operations. For example, local elected officials, companies you do business with, and the convenience store clerk, can be some of your best supporters. An open house and tour will be fun for your staff and the community.

EXTERNAL AUDIENCES

Assignment

During your off season or shoulder season, invite your community out for a familiarization tour of your operation. It can be a time-specific open house or an entire day to enjoy all that your operation has to offer. Encourage community members to bring their families and plan special games and events for children.

Technique #173

Remove Unnecessary Burdens Associated with Volunteering

Due diligence is needed before appointing an individual as a volunteer at your site. The safety of guests and fellow staff is the first priority. In addition, the individual must have the ability to properly represent your establishment. Therefore, a well-constructed volunteer application process is needed. Nevertheless, the application process should not be bogged down with "unnecessary burdens" because the process is unclear, confusing, or outdated.

Once volunteering, other systems should be in place to make the volunteering experience as efficient as possible such as clearly communicated scheduling procedures and adequate lead-times when scheduled.

EXTERNAL AUDIENCES

Assignment

Discuss with the team whether the volunteering process and procedures are efficient or in need of improvement. Address both the application process and methods used to communicate with and schedule the current volunteer pool. Meet with current volunteers and solicit their feedback on the process.

Technique #174

Actively Pursue Grant Funding

Ecotourism sites are sometimes eligible for various types of grant funding. Much of these funds are available through organizations and foundations committed to advancing environmental-related initiatives. Sites located in economically recessed regions are often eligible for an even wider pool of grant funding sources.[36]

EXTERNAL AUDIENCES

Assignment

Who on your team enjoys writing? Ask them to write at least two grant applications per year. Even if the site is not selected as the recipient of funding, the grant applications help increase the visibility of the attraction to important stakeholders.

Technique #175

Invite Newly Elected Officials to Visit

Regardless of political views or party affiliation, once someone is elected to office, his/her role is to represent the region's constituents. Therefore, following an election, whether it be at the town/city, county, or statewide-level, invite the newly elected official to visit your attraction. The purpose of this visit would be to better familiarize him/her with your offerings.

EXTERNAL AUDIENCES

Assignment

Decide whether the various invitations should be extended by telephone, by email, or by post. Perhaps a telephone call might be more appropriate at the local-level, whereas, an email or letter might be more suitable when inviting a state-level official.

If the official takes you up on your invitation, be sure to host a welcoming visit but also one that is representative of what other visitors receive. Extending too much special treatment or perks could be perceived as attempting to 'gift' a political figure in hopes of political favors. To reiterate, the overarching purpose of the visit is to better familiarize him/her with your offerings.

Technique #176

Prominently Display the Names of Leading Supporters

Engraved placards or inscribed bricks are two suggestions in which the names of your ecotourism attraction's most loyal supporters can be permanently displayed. Those honored can include financial donors (individuals, families, or organizations) who have crossed a certain threshold of funding support. Honorees can also include on-site volunteers who have attained a particular number of volunteer hours. Having such commemoration in place will not only reinforce your gratitude towards those supporters but will also help attract the friends and family members of them to your attraction.

EXTERNAL AUDIENCES

Assignment

Discuss with your team whether your site already permanently displays the names of supporters. If so, are the criteria clear and consistently applied for inclusion in the honor? Are the names displayed in an area that is visible to the public? Do the individuals and organizations honored know that they are honored?

On the other hand, if your site does not currently have such a recognition system in place, discuss how it should be designed. Who will take responsibility for implementation and management of the program?

Technique #177

Institute a Tree Commemoration Program

If you have adequate space, consider initiating a program in which local residents can plant a tree at your site along with a message placard commemorating a loved one. Such a program would be useful in forging stronger bonds and emotional attachment between your attraction and local residents. The program would need well-structured guidelines pertaining to details such as type and location of tree and placard. For example, a standard placard type and style should likely be used for all.[37]

EXTERNAL AUDIENCES

Assignment

Do you have an area of your site that could accommodate more trees? Are you certain that you will never need to disturb the trees in the identified area with future construction or utility-related work? Will the operation or sponsor take care of the tree until the tree becomes established? If the tree dies, will it be replaced by the operation or sponsor? Is the commemoration perpetual or will it have an end date?

Technique #178

Serve as a Venue for Charity Events

Serving as a venue for community blood drives, food drives, or other mission-compliant charity events is another way to involve the community. Organizations often need a place with a crowd to fulfill their donation goals. Hosting controversial or politically polarizing events can backfire which is why blood drives and food drives are safe, yet important causes to support by lending use of your site.

EXTERNAL AUDIENCES

Assignment

Reach out to your nearest blood bank, food bank, or other community organizations and form mutually beneficial relationships. Plan to have these events on a regular basis. Each party will advertise the event letting your community know that your operation cares.

Technique #179

Reinforce the Cultural Heritage of the Local Community

Celebrate your community within an hour's drive of the entrance to your operation by highlighting the industry, popular past times, or hobbies. In doing so, guests will enjoy learning about the local culture. Moreover, local residents will likely feel a sense of pride that the culture is being shared and may forge a stronger attachment to your site.

EXTERNAL AUDIENCES

Assignment

Select a signature aspect of your community and accent that heritage. For example, if the area is known for agriculture, perhaps have a tractor show. If it is known for producing maple syrup, then host a maple syrup festival. If textiles are part of the area's heritage, then display quilts that have been handcrafted locally. This connection with local heritage will create a sense of pride for the community and will add value to your visitors' experiences.

Technique #180

Have Physicians "Prescribe" Your Attraction

Due to the well-known health benefits associated with spending time in the outdoors, various programs have emerged in which physicians prescribe a visit to an outdoor setting as a remedy for certain ailments (e.g. obesity, high blood pressure). Park Rx America™ is an example of one such program. Such outdoor prescriptions expose new visitors to your site who might not have otherwise visited.[38]

EXTERNAL AUDIENCES

Assignment

Team to discuss this opportunity and decide what will be needed for possible implementation. Is there a regional, state, or national organization that represents your interest to elected and/or government officials? If so, encourage them to adopt this idea for more effectiveness.

Concluding Remarks

While the importance of the outdoors has always been appreciated by most, such importance was elevated during the global pandemic in recent years. Pictures and videos of people representing all walks of life could be seen walking, jogging, and bicycling while adhering to social distancing guidelines. The combination of fresh air and the sound of a bird singing is an immediate stress reliever.

Many of the readers of this book are entrusted with offering and managing some of the most culturally, historically, and naturally significant of these nature-based venues. This role is an honor. It is hoped that the information contained here will further elevate your ability to serve in this important role.

To learn more about the topics covered in this Handbook, please refer to the next section in which the latest research is sourced. In addition, if you have suggestions for the next edition of this Handbook, please let the authors know: Donald (www.tailgate-talks.com) and Vince (www.InstituteForServiceResearch.com). The authors would enjoy discussing these topics with you and your team.

Thank you and Good Luck!

Additional Resources, References, and Notes

[1] For more about the brand-signaling effects of signage, see for example:

Kellaris, J. J., & Machleit, K. A. (2016). Signage as marketing communication: A conceptual model and research propositions. *Interdisciplinary Journal of Signage and Wayfinding*, *1*(1).

Magnini, V. P., Miller, T., & Kim, B. (2011). The psychological effects of foreign-language restaurant signs on potential diners. *Journal of Hospitality & Tourism Research*, *35*(1), 24-44.

Sundar, A., Gonsales, F., & Schafer, G. (2018). Synchronicity in signage promotes a sense of belonging. *Interdisciplinary Journal of Signage and Wayfinding*, *2*(2), 30-40.

[2] As additional resources pertaining to the role of restroom cleanliness, see for instance:

Liu, P., & Lee, Y. M. (2018). An investigation of consumers' perception of food safety in the restaurants. *International Journal of Hospitality Management*, *73*, 29-35.

Kim, H., & Bachman, J. R. (2019). Examining customer perceptions of restaurant restroom cleanliness and their impact on satisfaction and intent to return. *Journal of Foodservice Business Research*, *22*(2), 191-208.

Ros, K., Mocanu, E., & Seifert, C. (2019). Airport Restroom Cleanliness Prediction Using Real Time User Feedback Data. In *1st IEEE International Conference on Cognitive Machine Intelligence*.

[3] Further research surrounding the importance of accessibility can be found here:

Eichhorn, V., & Buhalis, D. (2011). Accessibility: A key objective for the tourism industry. *Accessible Tourism: Concepts and Issues*, 46-61.

McLean, S. N. (2015). Are all tourist dependent businesses meeting their statutory obligations and taking full advantage of the entire economic value of the tourist budget (An investigation into statutory compliance for providing reasonable adjustment to facilitate equal access for disabled customers to goods and services). *Journal of Building Surveying Appraisal and Valuation*, *4*(3).

Wakiya, T. (2011). *Overcoming the barriers toward inclusive design of tourism* (Doctoral dissertation, University of Surrey (United Kingdom)).

[4] For more about the concept of parkitecture, see for example:

> Dunlap, T. R. (1999). Explorations in Environmental History: Essays by Samuel P. Hays.
>
> McCrimmon, L. (2016). A New 'Parkitecture': Re-Imagining the Interpretive Centre as an Interactive Route in Algonquin Provincial Park.
>
> Morrisey, E. K. (2014). *Parkitecture: Integrating Park Qualities Into Architecture* (Doctoral dissertation, Boston Architectural College).

[5] Additional information regarding trends surrounding RV camping, can be located here:

> Brochado, A., & Pereira, C. (2017). Comfortable experiences in nature accommodation: Perceived service quality in Glamping. *Journal of Outdoor Recreation and Tourism, 17,* 77-83.
>
> Brooker, E., & Joppe, M. (2013). Trends in camping and outdoor hospitality—An international review. *Journal of Outdoor Recreation and Tourism, 3,* 1-6.
>
> Lyu, S. O., Kim, J. W., & Bae, S. W. (2019). Family vacationers' willingness to pay for glamping travel sites: A family functioning segmentation. *International Journal of Tourism Research, 22*(2), 255-167.

[6] For example, the satisfaction difference between those who do and do not have staff interactions has been statistically significant since 2010 (the first year that it was measured):

> Magnini, V. (2020). Virginia State Parks: Your Comments Count Annual Report. Virginia Department of Conservation and Recreation: Richmond, Virginia.

[7] The concept of the drama metaphor was popularized, in part, by Disney when they began referring to their employees as "cast members." Some seminal writings on the topic are as follows:

> Fisk, R. P., & Grove, S. J. (1996). Applications of impression management and the drama metaphor in marketing: an introduction. *European Journal of Marketing, 30*(9), 6-12.
>
> Pine, B. J., Pine, J., & Gilmore, J. H. (1999). *The experience economy: Work is theatre & every business a stage.* Harvard Business Press.

[8] A study demonstrating the powerful effects of eye contact:

   Musicus, A., Tal, A., & Wansink, B. (2015). Eyes in the Aisles: Why Is Cap'n Crunch Looking Down at My Child?. *Environment and Behavior*, *47*(7), 715-733.

[9] Research summarizing face and name recall techniques:

   Magnini, V. P., & Honeycutt Jr, E. D. (2005). Face recognition and name recall: training implications for the hospitality industry. *Cornell Hotel and Restaurant Administration Quarterly*, *46*(1), 69-78.

[10] Research that demonstrates that thanking a visitor for providing constructive feedback improves visitor satisfaction:

   Magnini, V. P., & Karande, K. (2009). The influences of transaction history and thank you statements in service recovery. *International Journal of Hospitality Management*, *28*(4), 540-546.

[11] More about visitor surprise can be found here:

   Magnini, V. P. (2014). *Surprise!: The Secret to Customer Loyalty in the Service Sector*. Business Expert Press.

   Magnini, V. P., & Dallinger, I. (2018). Consumer information overload and the need to prompt script deviations. *Journal of Quality Assurance in Hospitality & Tourism*, *19*(3), 285-297.

[12] Further research surrounding the importance of smiling can be found here:

   Choi, S., Choi, C., & Mattila, A. S. (2020). Are All Smiles Perceived Equal? The Role of Service Provider's Gender. *Cornell Hospitality Quarterly* (in-press).

   Otterbring, T. (2017). Smile for a while: the effect of employee-displayed smiling on customer affect and satisfaction. *Journal of Service Management*, *28*(2), 284-304.

   Silva, L. A. (2018). How much is a smile worth? The effect of smiling faces in food retail stores. *Race: revista de administração, contabilidade e economia*, *17*(3), 841-850.

   Söderlund, M., & Rosengren, S. (2008). Revisiting the smiling service worker and customer satisfaction. *International Journal of Service Industry Management*, *19*(5), 552-574.

[13] The role of employer branding in recruiting is examined here:

> Botha, A., Bussin, M., & De Swardt, L. (2011). An employer brand predictive model for talent attraction and retention. *SA Journal of Human Resource Management*, 9(1), 1-12.
>
> Theurer, C. P., Tumasjan, A., Welpe, I. M., & Lievens, F. (2018). Employer branding: a brand equity-based literature review and research agenda. *International Journal of Management Reviews*, 20(1), 155-179.
>
> Wilden, R., Gudergan, S., & Lings, I. (2010). Employer branding: strategic implications for staff recruitment. *Journal of Marketing Management*, 26(1-2), 56-73.

[14] More about screening for emotional intelligence through interviewing can be found here:

> Christina, S. C., & Latham, G. P. (2004). The situational interview as a predictor of academic and team performance: A study of the mediating effects of cognitive ability and emotional intelligence. *International Journal of Selection and Assessment*, 12(4), 312-320.
>
> Kluemper, D. H., McLarty, B. D., Bishop, T. R., & Sen, A. (2015). Interviewee selection test and evaluator assessments of general mental ability, emotional intelligence and extraversion: Relationships with structured behavioral and situational interview performance. *Journal of Business and Psychology*, 30(3), 543-563.
>
> Magnini, V. P. (2014). *Surprise!: The Secret to Customer Loyalty in the Service Sector*. Business Expert Press.

[15] Panel-style interviewing has been a topic of research in peer-reviewed studies; for example:

> Dixon, M., Wang, S., Calvin, J., Dineen, B., & Tomlinson, E. (2002). The panel interview: A review of empirical research and guidelines for practice. *Public Personnel Management*, 31(3), 397-428.
>
> Levashina, J., Hartwell, C. J., Morgeson, F. P., & Campion, M. A. (2014). The structured employment interview: Narrative and quantitative review of the research literature. *Personnel Psychology*, 67(1), 241-293.
>
> Wilhelmy, A., Kleinmann, M., König, C. J., Melchers, K. G., & Truxillo, D. M. (2016). How and why do interviewers try to make impressions on applicants? A qualitative study. *Journal of Applied Psychology*, 101(3), 313.

[16] Research demonstrates that employer branding influences employee attraction; see for example:

> Kumari, S., & Saini, G. K. (2018). Do instrumental and symbolic factors interact in influencing employer attractiveness and job pursuit intention?. *Career Development International, 23*(4), 444-462.
>
> Sokro, E. (2012). Impact of employer branding on employee attraction and retention. *European Journal of Business and Management, 4*(18), 164-173.

[17] The linkage between empowerment and motivation can be seen here:

> Martin, S. L., Liao, H., & Campbell, E. M. (2013). Directive versus empowering leadership: A field experiment comparing impacts on task proficiency and proactivity. *Academy of Management Journal, 56*(5), 1372-1395.
>
> Seibert, S. E., Wang, G., & Courtright, S. H. (2011). Antecedents and consequences of psychological and team empowerment in organizations: A meta-analytic review. *Journal of Applied Psychology, 96*(5), 981.
>
> Zhang, X., & Bartol, K. M. (2010). Linking empowering leadership and employee creativity: The influence of psychological empowerment, intrinsic motivation, and creative process engagement. *Academy of Management Journal, 53*(1), 107-128.

[18] There is a large body of research about customers' heightened attention during/after a failure situation; for example:

> Gelbrich, K., & Roschk, H. (2011). A meta-analysis of organizational complaint handling and customer responses. *Journal of Service Research, 14*(1), 24-43.
>
> La, S., & Choi, B. (2012). The role of customer affection and trust in loyalty rebuilding after service failure and recovery. *The Service Industries Journal, 32*(1), 105-125.
>
> Magnini, V. P., Ford, J. B., Markowski, E. P., & Honeycutt, E. D. (2007). The service recovery paradox: justifiable theory or smoldering myth?. *Journal of Services Marketing, 21*(3), 213-225.

[19] More about the linkages between goal setting and motivation can be found here:

> Bronkhorst, B., Steijn, B., & Vermeeren, B. (2015). Transformational leadership, goal setting, and work motivation: The case of a Dutch municipality. *Review of Public Personnel Administration, 35*(2), 124-145.

Gómez-Miñambres, J. (2012). Motivation through goal setting. *Journal of Economic Psychology, 33*(6), 1223-1239.

Lunenburg, F. C. (2011). Goal-setting theory of motivation. *International Journal of Management, Business, and Administration, 15*(1), 1-6.

[20] Galati, A., Crescimanno, M., Tinervia, S., & Fagnani, F. (2017). Social media as a strategic marketing tool in the Sicilian wine industry: Evidence from Facebook. *Wine Economics and Policy, 6*(1), 40-47.

[21] More about social media marketing can be found here:

Alalwan, A. A., Rana, N. P., Dwivedi, Y. K., & Algharabat, R. (2017). Social media in marketing: A review and analysis of the existing literature. *Telematics and Informatics, 34*(7), 1177-1190.

Harrigan, P., Evers, U., Miles, M., & Daly, T. (2017). Customer engagement with tourism social media brands. *Tourism Management, 59*, 597-609.

Leung, X. Y., Bai, B., & Stahura, K. A. (2015). The marketing effectiveness of social media in the hotel industry: A comparison of Facebook and Twitter. *Journal of Hospitality & Tourism Research, 39*(2), 147-169.

Virtanen, H., Björk, P., & Sjöström, E. (2017). Follow for follow: marketing of a start-up company on Instagram. *Journal of Small Business and Enterprise Development, 24*(3), 468-484.

[22] For more about sensory messaging see, for instance:

Davis, E. A., Magnini, V. P., Weaver, P. A., & McGehee, N. G. (2013). The influences of verbal smell references in radio advertisements. *Journal of Hospitality & Tourism Research, 37*(2), 281-299.

Magnini, V. P., & Gaskins, J. N. (2010). Gender differences in responses to written touch references in hospitality print advertisements. *Tourism Analysis, 15*(3), 331-343.

Magnini, V. P., & Karande, K. (2010). An experimental investigation into the use of written smell references in ecotourism advertisements. *Journal of Hospitality & Tourism Research, 34*(3), 279-293.

[23] https://www.tripadvisor.com/TripAdvisorInsights/w828

[24] More about responding to TripAdvisor reviews can be found here:

> Min, H., Lim, Y., & Magnini, V. P. (2015). Factors affecting customer satisfaction in responses to negative online hotel reviews: The impact of empathy, paraphrasing, and speed. *Cornell Hospitality Quarterly, 56*(2), 223-231.

> Sparks, B. A., & Bradley, G. L. (2017). A "Triple A" typology of responding to negative consumer-generated online reviews. *Journal of Hospitality & Tourism Research, 41*(6), 719-745.

[25] For more information about the concept of social proof, see for example:

> Kenrick, D. T., Neuberg, S. L., Cialdini, R. B., & Professor Robert B. Cialdini. (2010). *Social psychology: Goals in interaction*. Boston, MA: Pearson.

> Magnini, V. P., Karande, K., Singal, M., & Kim, D. (2013). The effect of brand popularity statements on consumers' purchase intentions: The role of instrumental attitudes toward the act. *International Journal of Hospitality Management, 34*, 160-168.

> Salmon, S. J., De Vet, E., Adriaanse, M. A., Fennis, B. M., Veltkamp, M., & De Ridder, D. T. (2015). Social proof in the supermarket: Promoting healthy choices under low self-control conditions. *Food Quality and Preference, 45*, 113-120.

[26] Kolasa, J., & Zalewski, M. (1995). Notes on ecotone attributes and functions. Hydrobiologia, 303(1-3), 1-7.

[27] Research regarding individuals' propensity to recycle can be found here:

> Crociata, A., Agovino, M., & Sacco, P. L. (2015). Recycling waste: does culture matter?. *Journal of Behavioral and Experimental Economics, 55*, 40-47.

> Dilkes-Hoffman, L., Ashworth, P., Laycock, B., Pratt, S., & Lant, P. (2019). Public attitudes towards bioplastics–knowledge, perception and end-of-life management. *Resources, Conservation and Recycling, 151*, 104479.

> Orset, C., Barret, N., & Lemaire, A. (2017). How consumers of plastic water bottles are responding to environmental policies?. *Waste Management, 61*, 13-27.

[28] More about food handling and the prevention of food borne illnesses can be found here:

> Läikkö-Roto, T., & Nevas, M. (2014). Restaurant business operators' knowledge of food hygiene and their attitudes toward official food control affect the hygiene in their restaurants. *Food Control, 43*, 65-73.
>
> Manning, L. (2018). The value of food safety culture to the hospitality industry. *Worldwide Hospitality and Tourism Themes*.
>
> Martins, R. B., Hogg, T., & Otero, J. G. (2012). Food handlers' knowledge on food hygiene: The case of a catering company in Portugal. *Food Control, 23*(1), 184-190.

[29] Search and rescue foundational information and recent advances:

> Adams, A. L., Schmidt, T. A., Newgard, C. D., Federiuk, C. S., Christie, M., Scorvo, S., & DeFreest, M. (2007). Search is a time-critical event: when search and rescue missions may become futile. *Wilderness & Environmental Medicine, 18*(2), 95-101.
>
> Cooper, D. C., LaValla, P. H., & Stoffel, R. C. (1995). Search and rescue. *Wilderness Medicine: Management of Wilderness and Environmental Emergencies. St. Louis, MO: Mosby-Year Book*, 506-534.
>
> Grissom, C. K., Thomas, F., & James, B. (2006). Medical helicopters in wilderness search and rescue operations. *Air Medical Journal, 25*(1), 18-25.
>
> Norrington, L., Quigley, J., Russell, A., & Van der Meer, R. (2008). Modelling the reliability of search and rescue operations with Bayesian Belief Networks. *Reliability Engineering & System Safety, 93*(7), 940-949.
>
> Waharte, S., & Trigoni, N. (2010, September). Supporting search and rescue operations with UAVs. In *2010 International Conference on Emerging Security Technologies* (pp. 142-147). IEEE.

[30] The Society of Outdoor Recreation Professionals maintains a publicly-available library of state SCORPS:
https://www.recpro.org/scorp-library

[31] For more about visitation forecasting, please see:

Bartholomew, N. (2017). *Accurately predicting visitation as a strategic tool for management of a public park* (Doctoral dissertation, Kansas State University).

Clark, M., Wilkins, E. J., Dagan, D. T., Powell, R., Sharp, R. L., & Hillis, V. (2019). Bringing forecasting into the future: Using Google to predict visitation in US national parks. *Journal of Environmental Management, 243*, 88-94.

Snider, A. G. (2018). A general framework for gathering data to quantify annual visitation. *Journal of Park and Recreation Administration, 36*(1).

Wilmot, N. A., & McIntosh, C. R. (2014). Forecasting recreational visitation at US National Parks. *Tourism Analysis, 19*(2), 129-137.

[32] There is a well-established body of research covering the topic of perceived waiting times; for example:

Antonides, G., Verhoef, P. C., & Van Aalst, M. (2002). Consumer perception and evaluation of waiting time: A field experiment. *Journal of Consumer Psychology, 12*(3), 193-202.

Borges, A., Herter, M. M., & Chebat, J. C. (2015). "It was not that long!": The effects of the in-store TV screen content and consumers emotions on consumer waiting perception. *Journal of Retailing and Consumer Services, 22*, 95-106.

Luo, W., Liberatore, M. J., Nydick, R. L., Chung, Q. B., & Sloane, E. (2004). Impact of process change on customer perception of waiting time: a field study. *Omega, 32*(1), 77-83.

Mishalani, R. G., McCord, M. M., & Wirtz, J. (2006). Passenger wait time perceptions at bus stops: Empirical results and impact on evaluating real-time bus arrival information. *Journal of Public Transportation, 9*(2), 5.

Seawright, K. K., & Sampson, S. E. (2007). A video method for empirically studying wait-perception bias. *Journal of Operations management, 25*(5), 1055-1066.

[33] More about the economic impacts of ecotourism can be explored here:

Magnini, V. P., & Uysal, M. (2016). Virginia State Parks–Economic Impact Report. Blacksburg, VA.

Mules, T. (2005). Economic impacts of national park tourism on gateway communities: the case of Kosciuszko National Park. *Tourism Economics, 11*(2), 247-259.

Sandbrook, C. G. (2010). Local economic impact of different forms of nature-based tourism. *Conservation Letters, 3*(1), 21-28.

[34] More about interpretation can be found here:

Al-Busaidi, Y. Q. (2008). *Public interpretation of archaeological heritage and archaeotourism in the Sultanate of Oman* (Doctoral dissertation, University of Wales).

Benton, G. M. (2009). From Principle to Practice: Four Conceptions of Interpretation. *Journal of Interpretation Research, 14*(1).

Cadden, L. (2006). The common roots of environmental education and interpretation. *IN MY OPINION*, 39.

Petrtyl, B. R. (2013). Heritage Interpretation Versus the Greatest Crisis the National Park Service has Ever Known.

Phan, T. T. L., & Schott, C. (2019). Visitor responses to environmental interpretation in protected areas in Vietnam: a motivation-based segmentation analysis. *Tourism Recreation Research, 44*(4), 492-506.

Wearing, S., & Archer, D. (2003). An 'interpretation opportunity spectrum': a new approach to the planning and provision of interpretation in protected areas. *CAUTHE 2003: Riding the Wave of Tourism and Hospitality Research*, 1002.

[35] The connection between website accuracy and quality perceptions can be seen here:

Dragulanescu, N. G. (2002). Website quality evaluations: criteria and tools. *The International Information & Library Review, 34*(3), 247-254.

Mebrate, T. (2010). A framework for evaluating academic website's quality from students' perspective. Master's thesis: Delft, The Netherlands.

[36] More about applying for grants can be found here:

Demicheli, V., & Di Pietrantonj, C. (2005). Peer review for improving the quality of grant applications. *Cochrane Database of Systematic Reviews*, (2).

Nelson, D., & Ruffalo, L. (2017). Grant writing: Moving from generating ideas to applying to grants that matter. *The International Journal of Psychiatry in Medicine, 52*(3), 236-244.

Wood, F., & Wessely, S. (2003). Peer review of grant applications: a systematic review. In *Peer Review in Health Sciences*. BMJ Books.

[37] More about the use of trees for the purpose of commemoration can be found here:

McMillen, H. L., Campbell, L. K., & Svendsen, E. S. (2017). Co-creators of memory, metaphors for resilience, and mechanisms for recovery: Flora in living memorials to 9/11. *Journal of Ethnobiology, 37*(1), 1-20.

Sather-Wagstaff, J. (2015). Trees as reappropriated heritage in popular cultures of memorialization: The rhetoric of resilient (human) nature. In *Encounters with Popular Pasts* (pp. 235-250). Springer, Cham.

Stephens, J. (2009). Remembrance and commemoration through honour avenues and groves in Western Australia. *Landscape Research, 34*(1), 125-141.

[38] Connections between outdoor environments and health and well-being are demonstrated here:

Frumkin, H., Bratman, G. N., Breslow, S. J., Cochran, B., Kahn Jr, P. H., Lawler, J. J., ... & Wood, S. A. (2017). Nature contact and human health: A research agenda. *Environmental Health Perspectives, 125*(7), 075001.

https://parkrxamerica.org/ (accessed April 6, 2020).

Sandifer, P. A., Sutton-Grier, A. E., & Ward, B. P. (2015). Exploring connections among nature, biodiversity, ecosystem services, and human health and well-being: Opportunities to enhance health and biodiversity conservation. *Ecosystem Services, 12*, 1-15.

Thompson Coon, J., Boddy, K., Stein, K., Whear, R., Barton, J., & Depledge, M. H. (2011). Does participating in physical activity in outdoor natural environments have a greater effect on physical and mental wellbeing than physical activity indoors? A systematic review. *Environmental Science & Technology, 45*(5), 1761-1772.

Zhang, J. W., Piff, P. K., Iyer, R., Koleva, S., & Keltner, D. (2014). An occasion for unselfing: Beautiful nature leads to prosociality. *Journal of Environmental Psychology, 37*, 61-72.

Index

accessibility 28
accolades 67, 73, 109
after hours emergencies 159
again effect 55
applicant 67, 69-73
art contest 203
artifact 135
automated external defibrillator (AED) 157
awkward silence 61
bees 121
binoculars 33
bioblitz 118
blog 99
bottle filler 137
brand tagline 112
branding 112
buffer zones 26
butterflies 121
business cards 75
camper-to-camper interface 179
campground 31-33, 143, 159-160, 177, 179
carbon footprint 115, 138
carrying capacity 97, 120, 167
Chamber of Commerce 194
charity events 107, 212
civic organizations 194-195
Civilian Conservation Corps (U.S.) 29, 134
Children 37, 39, 58, 183, 203
climate change 115, 123
congestion points 167
consistent terminology 49
constructive feedback 56
contracted visitor service provider 186-188
conversational ability 72
credit card technology 165, 168
cultural heritage 191, 213
customer service 38, 87, 139, 160, 172
delegation 76
dietary needs 158
directions 165, 182-183
donors 210
drama metaphor 42
drone 94, 104
Earth Day 115, 136
economic impacts 74, 185, 193

ecosystem 115-138
ecotones 118
Educators' Advisory Board 198
elected officials 206
electric car charging station 138
electrical breakers 178
electrical receptacles 178
email marketing 97
emergency response 146-147
emotional intelligence 70
empowerment 76
encounter story 81
entrance 17, 43, 61, 145, 213
environmental consciousness 138
environmental education 115, 125, 130
environmental history 133
eye contact 51
Facebook 94
face-to-face encounters 41
failure recovery 79
familiarization (FAM) visits 100, 206
fauna 122, 125, 131-132
fencing 25
feedback 56, 85, 181
female appeal 98
festivals and events 68, 91, 97, 107-108, 139, 191, 201
fire 132, 156
first aid 157, 162
first time visitors 43, 60
flooding 132, 156
flora 118, 122, 125, 132
food borne illness 152
food service 169
forecast (visitation volumes) 172
forecast (weather) 53
fragrance 98
fresh eyes 38
garden club 107, 118
goals 84, 96-97, 165, 212
grant funding 208
gross domestic product 74, 193
group booking 201
helicopter landing zone (LZ) 147
holidays 83

hometown 78
hurricane 156
incident response system (ICS) 148
Instagram 95
interpretive programming 67, 123, 130, 133, 196
interview (of staff) 65, 69-73
invasive species 119
January 1st event 108
job announcements 67
jobs supported 74, 193
labor income 74, 193
length of stay 177
lighting 117, 126-127, 145
listening post mentality 181
live animal exhibit 131
live streaming 28, 97, 111, 198
living classroom 125
locally sourced materials 128
lost visitor 22, 139, 153-154
map 22, 26, 118, 124, 133-134, 175, 182
marketing ROI survey 113
medical needs 158-159
mirrors 77, 173
motivating staff 65, 74-86
movie theaters 45
mowing 115, 121
mud slide 156
multiple day interview 69
must see 43
nametag 78
native inhabitants 205
natural disaster 139, 156
natural screening 24
non-verbal cues 38, 41, 59
off-site interpretation 130, 191, 196
on-call telephone system 160
orientation (of new staff) 50, 55, 88
pandemic 41, 196, 215
panel-style interview 72
parking 20, 30, 32, 141-142, 144-145, 151, 197
Parkitecture 29
performance evaluations 85
personal flotation device (PFD) 155
pets 18
photo 25, 29, 34-35, 47, 106, 199-200
photo contest 106
photo frame 34

photocell 127
physicians prescribe 214
physically fit 37
postage 52
postcards 52
rainy day option 183
real-time informational capability 44
recognition program 79, 86, 210
recruitment (of staff) 67, 88
reclaimed 128
recycle 125, 128-129, 138
remembering names 55
resource allocation decisions 170
restoration 124
restroom 18, 23
roadway markings 142
RV camper 30-31, 170, 176-178
safety equipment 155
satisfaction survey 86, 91
Saugatuck 112
scavenger hunt 58
seamless experience delivery 88, 189
seasonal staff 88-89
search and rescue 154
search engine optimization (SEO) 103
seed 122
selecting staff 65, 69-73
sensory messaging 98
setting the stage 15-38
shopping malls 45
signs 17, 19-22, 35, 141-142, 151, 165, 175
slip and fall incident 139, 163
smell 98, 143
smiling 57, 59
social media 34, 91, 93-96, 106, 109-110
solar 127
staff meeting 80-83
Statewide Comprehensive Outdoor Recreation Plan (SCORP) 170
Strategic alliances 191,202
strategic plan 185
surprise story 82
take / leave station 129
tax revenue 74, 193
teamwork 87
telephone 27, 57, 159, 201, 209
telephone charging station 27
ten foot rule 50

text messaging 174
thank you 17, 53, 56, 63
theme parks 45
tornado 156
touch 98, 117
trail 22, 35, 37, 144
travel writers 105
treasure chest 58
tree commemoration program 211
tree hazards 144
TripAdvisor 99, 101, 109
tripping hazards 149
tsunami 156
Twitter 95
typhoon 156
uniforms 77, 89
unique natural occurrences 111
verbal cues 59
veteran 197
video 71, 94, 104, 138, 200

viewshed 35-36
VIP treatment 197
Virginia State Parks 112
vision statement 188
visitor requests 171
visitor satisfaction 28, 87, 91, 165, 184, 186
volunteers 119, 154, 199, 210
wagons 32
waiting times 173
water fountain 137
weather forecast 53
website 28, 37, 53, 91, 103-104, 114, 138, 200-201
website traffic 114
web analytics 114
Wikipedia 102
wildlife encounters 161
word-of-mouth 93
Zoom technology 41, 196

NOTES

About the Authors

Donald V. Forgione has nearly four decades of progressive leadership experience in the tourism, hospitality, environmental, and parks & recreation fields. He understands what it takes to foster a top-rate customer service culture while protecting the natural and cultural resources. His passion for the land and her people is inspiring and contagious.

He has held many positions from Park Ranger to the former Director of Florida's Park System which includes 1,800 employees, 27,000 volunteers, $137M annual budget, and 174 parks. Under Donald's leadership, the Florida Park Service was awarded the National Gold Medal for Excellence making Florida the only state to win this prestigious accolade four times.

A sought-after consultant and speaker in the ecotourism industry, Donald is the Executive Director of *Tailgate Talks*: www.tailgate-talks.com

Vincent P. Magnini, Ph.D. was recently ranked as one of the top 12 most prolific hospitality researchers worldwide and holds editorial board appointments on nearly all of the top-ranked hospitality research journals in the field. Further, he is a U.S. Fulbright Scholar. He has published seven books and more than 250 articles and reports. Vince has also been featured on National Public Radio's (NPR) *All Things Considered, With Good Reason, Pulse on the Planet* and cited in the *New York Times* and *Washington Post*.

For nearly 20 years, Vince has been conducting customer experience surveying, economic impact modeling, program evaluations, and designing strategic plans for park systems, hotels, and private attractions.

An international lecturer and speaker, he is the Executive Director of the *Institute for Service Research*: www.InstituteForServiceResearch.com